PRAISE FOR **THE WISDOM O**ı **ᴛ**ᴴᴱ **COUNCIL**

"The Wisdom of The Council inspires the reader to manifest their extraordinary goals and make them possible. Sara Landon acts as the channel for The Council, whose messages and information have helped benefit and transform the lives of so many across the world. Sara is one of the great channelers of our times!"

– **Kevin Moore**, host of *The Moore Show* and *They Call Us Channelers*

"A transcendent vibration of unconditional love can be felt within every page of *The Wisdom of The Council*. It's the kind of love that can move mountains and heal worlds. Sara has dedicated her life to doing inner work that has allowed her to be a pure vessel who embodies and brings forth transcendent wisdom into the world. This book serves as a reminder of the magnificence that you are and have always been."

– **Emmanuel Dagher**, author of *Easy Breezy Prosperity* and *Easy Breezy Miracle*

"If you know that there is something bigger within yourself that is ready to be created but just can't put your finger on it, this is the book for you. Sara Landon and The Council will expertly, expeditiously, and lovingly guide you to discovering your purpose and living to your highest potential. It is a guidebook whose time has come: the next generation of a genre of channeled wisdom that will open the doorway to your embodied awareness of the life you are ready for and capable of creating."

– **John Burgos**, creator and host of *Beyond the Ordinary Show*

"The Council's teachings are an integral part of my life. They are a source of guidance and inspiration, but it goes so far beyond their words; their communication is a vibrational experience capable of transforming the human mental, emotional, and energetic state. Loving, humorous, and wise, The Council is here to help the collective usher in an awakened planet and help each of us live a life of peace, joy, freedom, and purpose. I am thrilled to see their wisdom now embodied in book form in *The Wisdom of The Council*."

– **Sunny Joy McMillan**, author of *Unhitched* and host of *Sunny in Seattle*

"The most precious moments in life are those when you're undeniably in the presence of Truth. Those moments can bring tears to your eyes, joy to your heart, and a deep knowing in your soul. That is precisely how I experience being with The Council. Their message goes far beyond words on a page. Whether you are a lifelong seeker or are just now opening into the deeper truths of life, *The Wisdom of The Council* is a direct path to becoming everything you wish to be."

– **Dr. Curt Eastin**, personal development and energy psychology coach

"The Council's teachings are simple yet uncommon. Sara is the perfect choice on the planet to bring forth this wisdom for humanity. Heaven is a consciousness you tune in to, not a place you go. The results you'll experience from living this wisdom will be extraordinary. This isn't a promise; it's a guarantee!"

– **Danny Khursigara**, co-author of *The Road to Success*

"Every page, every word holds the vibrational frequency of pure love. As you read and re-read this profound wisdom from The Council, your body will recognize and resonate with its truth, not only within these pages, but the truth that resides within you. This book will lovingly guide you into the realization of just how powerful you are to create the life you want to live."

– **Fiona Paul**, intuitive guide and channel

"Bravo! A brilliant and beautiful book of Divine guidance that lights the way to the New Earth. *The Wisdom of The Council* gifts readers with life-changing wisdom and simple principles toward creating an abundant, joyful, purpose-filled life. Within its pages are the answers to every question, but perhaps more importantly, the elevated perspective that enables us to step into our true power as the Creators we were born to be. The Council lovingly takes readers on the journey to mastery, leaving one empowered, equipped, and excited to fully embrace these extraordinary times in which we live."

– **Lyn White**, director of Animals International

THE
WISDOM
OF THE
COUNCIL

THE
WISDOM
OF THE
COUNCIL

CHANNELED
MESSAGES FOR
LIVING YOUR
PURPOSE

SARA LANDON

HAY HOUSE, INC.
Carlsbad, California • New York City
London • Sydney • New Delhi

Published in the United States by: Hay House, Inc.: www.hayhouse.com®
Published in Australia by: Hay House Australia Pty. Ltd.: www.hayhouse.com.au
Published in the United Kingdom by: Hay House UK, Ltd.: www.hayhouse.co.uk
Published in India by: Hay House Publishers India: www.hayhouse.co.in

Project editor: Anna Cooperberg
Cover design: Barbara LeVan Fisher
Interior design: Karla Schweer

Cataloging-in-Publication Data is on file with the Library of Congress

Tradepaper ISBN: 978-1-4019-7045-1
E-book ISBN: 978-1-4019-7046-8
Audiobook ISBN: 978-1-4019-7047-5

10 9 8 7 6 5 4 3 2 1
1st edition, November 2022

Printed in the United States of America

This book is dedicated to all of you who desire to live your highest potential and master your life experience. You have drawn this book to you at this time because you are ready to truly live as the master that you are. Not as a master over any other, but a master because you have realized a level of consciousness, awareness, energy, vibration, thought forms, and creation that allows you the freedom to choose any reality, any experience, and any expression of all that you are.

May the wisdom and teachings within this book guide you to the realization of who you really are, why you are here, and all that is possible for you in this magnificent human experience.

CONTENTS

Foreword **xi**
Introduction **1**
An Opening Message from the Council **15**

CHAPTER ONE
Celebrate Your Magnificent Transformation **23**

CHAPTER TWO
I Am the Master, I Am the Magic, I Am the Miracle **33**

CHAPTER THREE
Step into the I Am Creator Frequency **47**

CHAPTER FOUR
The Path of the Wayshower **59**

CHAPTER FIVE
The Most Extraordinary Life Imaginable **77**

CHAPTER SIX
Living in Harmony with Your Destiny **91**

CHAPTER SEVEN
Awaken within the Dream 107

CHAPTER EIGHT
Let the Light Guide the Way 125

CHAPTER NINE
Navigating Current Events with Peace and Grace 141

CHAPTER TEN
The Potential for a Fully Awakened World 159

CHAPTER ELEVEN
Impeccable Creation of a Richer, Fuller Experience 173

CHAPTER TWELVE
The Powerful Creator That You Are 185

Afterword 201
About the Author 203

FOREWORD

"Who am I?" is the quintessential question at the heart of every philosophical pursuit and the basis for the sense of wonder we feel about our very existence. This universal question, echoed from the Himalayas to Hollywood by yogis, shamans, and seekers, has been presumed rhetorical. However, believing as I do that in the purest sense there is an absolute truth to all things—I believe this question not only has an answer, but that the answer lies within these very pages.

This truth, as you'll find, is electrifying. It is bursting with the unexpected possibilities that await each of us for living happier, longer, and more fulfilled lives.

I met Sara Landon in 2019 and shortly thereafter had a private session with The Council, who spun my mind in every direction before turning it inside out. Among other personal revelations, they informed me that my lifelong suspicion that each of us can fully self-realize à la Jesus Christ, Buddha, and other enlightened masters was indeed possible. In fact, once "the work" has been done, it's inevitable. And "the work" for many of us was done long ago in countless unremembered lifetimes. They shared that to them, *enlightenment* meant transcending life's illusions (time, space, and matter) by understanding *our* nature to live consciously and deliberately.

Note that it's not transcendence to dispel the illusions as some sort of spiritual endgame. Rather, transcendence means to recognize and view these illusions with a proper perspective, enabling us to live *among them* with a joy that would otherwise be completely unimaginable. It is a transcendence that banishes fear, turns illness into health, lack into abundance, confusion into clarity, and loneliness into friendships in this love-game we call life. And yes, if you also wanted to walk on water or ascend, you could do that too.

The words of The Council are unequivocal: You are divine, capable of living the life you dream of in a world that exists *for you*. That you are *of* God, *by* God, and *pure* God. You are born to thrive, pushed on to greatness every day of your life, surrounded by elements that unceasingly look to you for direction. That joy is not only possible for every single one of us, but it's ultimately assured, and its manifestation is why we chose this—and every—lifetime.

To explore the final frontier of the universe and our existence in order to go where very few have gone, the questions are, "How do I fully awaken?" and then, "What shall I do with my sacred adventure into form, alive in this mind-boggling paradise of splendor?" Both of which, again, are supremely answerable, and are similarly contained herein. To cut to the chase of the second answer, you will soon read that you can do, be, and have absolutely anything you can dream of, and even far more than you can dream of.

Also shared within is an extraordinary view of the times in which we find ourselves, especially for those reading these words prior to the global transformation now upon us:

Your destiny is that of a master. It is, or you wouldn't be reading this. You are here to help guide your beloved human family through the greatest awakening of human consciousness that has ever occurred on your planet. You are here to illuminate the potential for humankind.

Finally, the old cliche of "all things are possible" has new clarity, becoming more literal than whimsical.

You have chosen *this* existence, at *this* time, first, to discover who you really are, and second, to see where it leads you and the Earth's collective of natural-born Creators. You wield a power so great it can literally move mountains, bestow fortunes, and manifest thy divine will on Earth.

That this book is in your hands means that a tipping point has been reached in your own search for answers and very soon you will better understand what it means to have dominion over all things.

There's a new era dawning on planet Earth for which you are a pioneer. Legions will follow and marvel at the chasm you're about to cross as the world emerges from a millennia of ignorance into the light of truth—holding on to a vision that was impossible to see, following voices that are not of this realm, relying on instinct and possessing a courage that is your forgotten inheritance—to land surefooted and triumphant on this magnificent jewel hurtling through the cosmos: Heaven on Earth. Prophecies and legend, fulfilled.

The hard part has been done.

What now remains is putting the last few pieces of the puzzle together and easing into the sublime truth of your nature. To come fully alive in this very Garden of Eden. Where your thoughts become tangible things, your words give you wings, and your wish is the command of the entire universe.

Thy kingdom has come.

> —Mike Dooley
> *New York Times* best-selling author of *Infinite Possibilities* and *The Complete Notes from the Universe*

INTRODUCTION

*Live this wisdom and you will have a life
beyond your wildest dreams.*

— THE COUNCIL

Little did I know how fortuitous those words would be. Nor could I have ever predicted the transformation that would occur within and around me in the months and years to come. It truly was beyond anything I could have dreamed of.

My first experience with higher wisdom was not actually with The Council. Yet in hindsight, I see precisely how divinely orchestrated events were preparing me throughout my entire life to be a channel for their message to the world. I never desired to be a channel, but now I can't imagine my life any other way.

I grew up in a loving Christian family in a small town. As a child, I attended Sunday school each week and sang about God and Jesus's love. We prayed before family meals, praised the Lord, and kept Jesus in our hearts. I had a love for God and an awareness of my spiritual connection from a young age.

When I was seven years old, my parents divorced. My mother and I moved out of state, closer to her family. From the moment I first met my aunt Sunnie, my mother's sister, I remember being fascinated by her. She spoke about the soul, the power of the mind, the supernatural, and her master teacher, Mafu. Sunnie would explain that Mafu was a highly evolved being that was channeled through a young woman named Penny. She would tell me stories for hours about her recollections of past lives, soulmates, miracles, and the teachings of Mafu.

I first heard Mafu speak while watching a video with Sunnie. I was instantly captivated. There was an electrifying connection to the voice and the words that were spoken. It was as if Mafu's words were something that I knew, and I felt a resonant buzzing throughout my body.

I can also remember how devastated I felt the first time I overheard my family poking fun at my aunt for believing *that stuff.*

"How fake and phony," they would say.

On one occasion, when I was about 10 years old, I remember a close family member saying to me, "If she believes in that stuff, she will go to hell—and so will you, if you believe it."

It severed a cord deep within my heart. How could they say that about her? And what kind of God would do that? That day, I felt the light within me go out.

Over the years, I continued to listen to Mafu's audio and video tapes and read books about spirituality, past lives, and other metaphysical teachings. Yet after that day, I rarely ever spoke about it to anyone but my aunt. As I got older, I stopped using the words *God* and *Jesus.* I could not believe that the loving God I had sung about for all those years would damn someone like my aunt—or me—to hell.

On another occasion, I remember being told that people who do not accept Jesus in their hearts were going to hell.

I asked, "What about people in Indigenous tribes or remote places in the world who've never heard of Jesus? Are they going to hell?"

To which I was told, "Yes, that's what the Bible says."

Conflicted and overwhelmed by the contradiction between these ideas and what I was taught originally about a loving God, I lost interest in religion. I soon discovered personal development and cultivated a passion for achievement and life success. My focus became setting goals, starting my career, and climbing the corporate ladder. I was satiated by the desire to succeed and build a prosperous life.

Yet I would continually find myself reading books on spirituality and metaphysics. I was still searching for answers about life, God, Heaven and hell, truth, and the meaning of it all. Many years went by during which I considered myself an atheist despite knowing there was more to life than just living and dying.

That is, until one blistering cold winter day in November 2001—a day that would forever change the course of my life. I remember the heaviness in the room as I walked in to view the body of my deceased brother, Tim. He had been killed in a car accident the previous day. My family and I had flown to Alaska where he had been living. I had never seen a dead body, nor could I wrap my brain around my brother being gone. As I touched him, I was shocked by the cold, hard texture of his lifeless body. I immediately wanted to get away, and made my way over to a chair on the far side of the room.

I felt numb as I sat listening to the quiet sobbing of my mother and other family members. I can't tell you exactly how long I sat there. It felt like hours, but I am sure it was only minutes. Suddenly and unexpectedly, I felt this sense of peace wash over me. I began to feel a warm sensation of energy—like liquid love—flowing down from the crown of my head and into my entire body. I was completely and totally at peace and surrounded by a sense of love.

Then over my right shoulder I heard my brother say to me, *"I am still here. I am just not in there,"* referring to his body.

In my mind, I replied, *"Where are you?"*

"I am just as here as I ever was. I just left the density of the body. I am at a frequency that your physical senses cannot interpret," he replied. Although his words seemed strange, I understood.

My immediate next question was, *"Are you in Heaven?"*

To which he replied, *"Heaven and hell aren't like that. They are only experiences one has on Earth. There is only love here."*

Then as spontaneously as it began, the energy receded and the communication stopped. I was back in the cold room. Looking around at my family, it was clear that no one except me had heard Tim. In that moment I felt absolute peace about my brother's death, yet longed to speak with him again.

I didn't tell anyone about the conversation. Within a few days, I started to doubt that it really happened and began to question whether I had made it all up. But I could not deny what I felt or forget what he said.

Again and again, I attempted to reconnect to my brother and summon that warm liquid-love feeling. For many weeks, nothing happened. Then one day, as I was walking into the elevator at my office on the way back from lunch, I started to feel warm all over, and my hands began to tingle. There was no one in the elevator but me and a man I had never seen before. Over my right shoulder, I heard my brother say, *"Ask him his name."*

"I am not asking him his name," I responded mentally. But he persisted and again told me to ask the man his name.

Feeling a bit ridiculous, but doing as Tim said, I asked the man his name.

"Tim," he said, and then casually walked out the open doors of the elevator. Tim is my brother's name, I thought! This *is* real!

These types of experiences continued for years. My brother would spontaneously drop in with a message over my right shoulder. It was always preceded by a deep feeling of peace and love, and I soon began to know when he was there. I didn't know at the time (as I do now) how to connect with him intentionally or deliberately, but I felt comforted to know he was with me.

Some years later, at the height of my professional career, I started having strange experiences in the middle of the night. I would wake up and feel consumed by the desire to write. I had no memory of what I was writing and no idea from where the writing came.

In the morning, I would read what I'd written. It was certainly not information that I knew, and it wasn't written in the way that I usually spoke. The handwriting was noticeably different than my own. It contained the answers to my deepest questions about life, existence, God, and the universe. The writing was so beautiful, so loving, so wise. I couldn't summon the writing on command, but it continued spontaneously for several months. I now know this is an experience referred to as *automatic writing.*

Other strange things started to happen. I would look at a clock as it would read 1:11, 11:11, 2:22, 3:33, 4:44, 5:55. I started finding feathers when out on walks. I began to feel a deep love for flowers, birds, and animals. For seemingly no apparent reason, I would become overwhelmed with feelings of blissfulness and love. I felt one with everything and everyone, and would often know what people were going to say before they said it. I would begin to think of a friend or loved one and within minutes, they would call.

And while I felt such love and oneness, I would equally and as strongly feel a deep sense of sadness about the human experience and the suffering in the world. One moment I was immersed in love, peace, joy, and oneness, and the next minute I felt hopeless and lost. It was as if I had the wisdom of the world within me but no idea about my purpose or how to live it.

Several months later, I met a woman in hot yoga. I had noticed her in class a couple of days in a row. On the third day, I introduced myself. I asked her how she liked yoga and she replied, "I had to give it a try, but I am never coming back."

I laughed, not surprised, and asked her what she did. She explained she was a practitioner of Quantum Hypnosis Healing Technique. "What?" I asked.

She explained that she helped people communicate with their higher selves and connect to information from the other side. Intrigued, and hoping she could help me figure out what was going on in my life, I scheduled a session with her.

A few days later, she came to my house for the QHHT session. She led me through a guided meditation and then asked, "Do we have permission to talk with Sara's higher self?"

I said, "Yes," and she began to ask questions. We continued until suddenly my entire body was flooded with energy even beyond the warm liquid love. It was like nothing I had ever felt. It was like being shocked with volts of love, bliss, and ecstasy.

My hands and feet were tingling, and I felt a lightness—as if I was floating. My voice began to change, and I noticed that I had an accent and was speaking very quickly. I would later describe it like the voice of an Eastern European man. The peculiar voice coming through me went on speaking for over an hour. I was aware of myself but also aware that it wasn't *me* talking. I didn't remember what was said, but I could feel the truth and love in the words that were coming through. Luckily, the session had been recorded.

Afterward, I felt amazing. I could barely sleep that night. I was so energized and eager to replay the recording. As I listened to the peculiar voice, I realized the information being spoken was the same as what had been coming through in my writings months before. I was intrigued and excited, but also determined that no one would ever hear the replay of me talking in that strange voice.

The knowledge contained in the recording, however, was so profound that I just had to have another QHHT session. Again, the peculiar voice came through, only this time I was present for the entire conversation. Although I couldn't clearly remember everything, I was aware of what the voice was saying. On many occasions, the voice referred to itself as *we* or *us*.

Over time we began to call the voice The Council, as it seemed to be a group of wise, old souls providing answers to our many questions, thereby expanding our awareness. We continued with weekly sessions. Each time, more of my consciousness was present to the conversation. Eventually, I was fully aware of the information that was coming through me from The Council. Their messages felt like the deepest truth I had ever known, and as if I were remembering something I already knew.

THE COUNCIL'S FOUNDATIONAL TEACHINGS

The wisdom of The Council and its impact is multifaceted. Their unique perspective, their sometimes unusual way of saying things, and their obvious love for us affects us in many ways. Those of us compelled by their wisdom, however, find the *truths* they bring forward to be the most impactful when used as a guide to living well. These truths include:

- You are already everything you wish to be.

- You are the Creator within your own creation of reality.

- Life is meant to be joyful.

- What you focus on and the meaning you give it is what creates your reality.

- Consciousness moves energy into form; this is the formula for all creation.

- There is only love.

- Everything is always happening *for* you, not *to* you.

- You are Source Energy that *you* focused into a physical body.

- If you want to experience anything in the world around you, you must first create it within yourself.

- You have everything you need within you—and an infinite supply of resources—to create the life of your dreams.

- You have come here by your own choosing from an expanded state of consciousness to experience life (energy) in physical form.

- Life is a grand adventure and the journey only continues on from here.

- All of your power is in the now moment.

- Stillness is the access point to acceleration.

- There is no need to make big decisions about anything; allow all things to be *choiceless*.

- As you align to a higher level of consciousness, your well-being and abundance are assured.

- True Creation has no agenda.

- You get more of what you *are,* not what you *want.* If you want more joy in your life, align to the joy that is already within you and around you.

- When you are resisting anything, you are resisting everything and stopping the flow of easy, effortless, harmonious creation.

I had an absolute knowing of these truths when I first heard them despite having no idea how to live them. While each session with The Council always felt so pure, blissful, and loving, in my mind I could hear the words of my Christian family telling me that I would go to hell if I believed this stuff. I kept hearing all the things they said about my aunt Sunnie and Penny, the woman who channeled Mafu. I now imagined them saying those things about me. More than anything, I feared losing the love and admiration of my dad. I just knew he would not understand.

For almost a year, I continued doing sessions but told almost no one of The Council. We recorded hundreds of hours of information. I had the recordings transcribed and would read and reread every session. The wisdom and teachings were positively transforming every aspect of my life. Still, I had no idea what to do with all the information.

My only desire was to consume The Council's wisdom, walk my dogs, and spend time in nature. By this point, and to the shock of most all of my friends, family, and co-workers, I had resigned from my flourishing corporate career. I began meditating daily and within minutes could feel The Council's love and my consciousness merging with theirs. However, I want to emphasize that I never experience The Council as outside of me or as if they are taking me over. My connection with The Council occurs because I connect to a frequency *within me* that allows me to expand my awareness into higher levels of consciousness, which have always been there and available to me.

As time went on, I began spending hours translating the streams of thought that I was receiving daily through my connection to them. After some months of writing, I started recording voice communications. I had no idea why I was doing this, but I just trusted it, because it felt like what I was meant to do.

I had no plans to ever tell anyone about The Council. I didn't want people to think I was weird or woo-woo, but at the same time, I knew that I had to get The Council's powerful teachings to others and allow them to experience the transformation for themselves. Despite my trepidation, I offered sessions to a couple of close friends. Those sessions were profound and moving. They began to describe their experience as *a feeling of coming home, the gift of a lifetime, and the truth they had been searching for their entire lives.* Each person I shared The Council with began to experience rapid and miraculous transformations and manifestations in their lives. Within a few short years, I was doing sessions with The Council for people all over the world by phone.

The wisdom of The Council has now expanded into courses, books, seminars, summits, retreats, and a global community of people living The Council's wisdom and teachings. And I live a life beyond my wildest dreams, just as they assured me I would. Through the integration of The Council's wisdom, my life has more love, joy, abundance, freedom, well-being, and harmony than I ever thought possible.

I also now understand the original intention of the teachings of the Bible and the Christian religion. My own personal relationship with Jesus is one of love, appreciation, and continual presence in my life. I believe Jesus to be a great master whose wisdom came from the same origin and consciousness as that of The Council.

What's more, my greatest fear never materialized; my family has supported me in miraculous ways, and many now listen to The Council daily. My relationship with my dad is more loving and meaningful than ever before. He even shared with me that he had the same experience as I did with Tim when his father passed away. The night of my grandfather's death, my dad was lying in bed when suddenly he felt total peace and heard my grandfather say, *"Be in peace. All is well. I am here."* My father told me in that moment he was relieved of all his grief and sadness.

I believe that each of us has the ability to tune into higher wisdom and connect into the infinite field of consciousness in us and all around us in every moment. Whether your desire is to communicate with your higher self, a loved one on the other side, or the collective consciousness of your guides, I assure you, this is possible for you. Some years ago, I was guided to begin teaching others how to communicate with higher levels of consciousness. To date, I have taught more than four thousand people how to channel. Anyone can do this. It is not a power that only a few have; it is a natural and inherent ability that we never intended to forget.

My desire to discover my truth, my purpose, and the meaning of life is what summoned the consciousness of The Council. If you are reading this now, I can say the same for you. You drew this book and The Council to you. As they say, you would not be drawn to the vibration and frequency contained within these channeled messages if you yourself were not also a channel of divine love and higher wisdom—a part of The Council on Earth.

I've dedicated countless hours to channeling The Council's wisdom and sharing their messages to all who are ready to receive them. These are my deepest, heartfelt wishes for you:

May you remember the infinite wisdom that lies within you.

May you reconnect with the light that you are.

May you realize yourself as the powerful Creator that you are within your own creation of reality.

I am devoted to living The Council's profound, life-changing wisdom each and every day and I welcome you to join me on this incredible journey. This book is my gift to the world, and creating it has been an experience beyond my wildest dreams. It is my greatest joy to share The Wisdom of The Council with you.

WHO IS THE COUNCIL?

You are us. We are you. We come forth because we promised we would. So that you never forget who you really are, why you are here, and what you intended when you chose this magnificent life experience!

—The Council

While any description that can be understood by the human mind is tremendously limited, the brief answer is: The Council is a collective of Ascended Master beings with a higher level of consciousness and a grander perspective of the human experience.

Originally summoned by my asking to know my true purpose, The Council came forth over time as I allowed a greater connection with non-physical energy through a series of meaningful life events. Now The Council's profound wisdom is expressed readily, as I am able to simply relax and allow their perspective to flow through me.

Since first appearing in written and spoken words, their messages have expanded in response to the questions of a much larger group. Their powerful teachings continually become richer and deeper as the collective listening audience experiences life and desires more.

The Council is here to remind us of our own wisdom, which we never intended to forget.

WHAT IS CHANNELING?

If you are reading this, you almost certainly believe that there is more to life than what you experience with your physical senses. Perhaps you think of your unseen dimension as a soul or higher self and that of a greater power such as God, the Source, or another name that resonates with you.

No matter what terminology a person may use, the non-physical forces moving in our world are known, felt, and expressed in a wide variety of ways. One of these is known as channeling.

Generally, channeling refers to the translation of higher consciousness and a greater perspective into language. It is a means by which the non-physical communicates in our physical world. While not everyone deliberately receives infinite intelligence and translates it into words as a channel does, channeling is similar to things like hunches, intuitions, and flow that most of us experience each day.

Everyone opens up to broader perspectives in unique, personal ways. There is no requirement, no specific process, and you do not even need to have a conscious awareness of what is happening.

You do not have to meditate to get into such an expanded state, and you do not need to live on a mountaintop to have a spiritually rich life.

At the heart of channeling is the ability to open up to something more than the limited human self. This happens in countless ways for us when we are present—and with practice, it can happen more. Channeled connections are often easy to recognize in creative expressions like writing, painting, dancing, and other artistic mediums, but they occur in every area of life. Such creativity is often referred to as *inspired* because it seems to come from another place.

We've all seen examples of performances that seem to go beyond human capabilities. Athletes when they are "in the zone" and first responders during a crisis are good examples of this type of transcended experience. Still, there are many other instances of people opening up to a higher state of being that are easily overlooked because they are so common.

Can you think of a time when you were in the flow, when it felt like your day was magical and everything unfolded perfectly without any effort on your part?

Have you ever said something to someone that you know was brilliant, but you had no idea where it came from or how you knew it was the perfect thing to say?

Have you ever created a delicious meal without a recipe or even a plan and had it turn out to be one of the best meals you have ever experienced?

Do you ever move through traffic so harmoniously that it is as if some part of you knows what all the other drivers are going to do before they do it?

These may seem like frivolous examples, but they illustrate that we are readily connected to our higher self and the transcendent experiences this connection can bring. Channeling is merely allowing this greater aspect of us to express itself freely, and, truly, it is a very natural thing.

Whether you identify with these specific experiences or terms is not important. You can live in full connection with all that you are—a so-called master in this modern world—anytime you wish.

HOW TO USE THIS BOOK

This book carries within it higher levels of consciousness. While the words are important, this is a vibrational experience. As you read these words, feel a sense of being uplifted and notice an expansion of your awareness and how this feels in your body. Some describe it as "remembering."

We begin by addressing the most fundamental of The Council's teachings and truths and progress to how to live this wisdom day to day. Each of the 12 chapters addresses a key area of The Council's teachings, and the truths contained within them.

A note about The Council's unique dialogue: The Council uses words like *enoughness* and *choiceless* in sometimes uncommon ways. At first you might question the meaning of the words and how The Council uses them, but as you read and reread, you will begin to understand the perfection of their meaning. The Council also uses words like *wealth* and *richness*. These are meant to reflect an abundance of *every* kind of resource—not just money but connections, opportunities, ideas, creativity, time, energy, and much more. These words are not at all intended to describe financial stature or "net worth."

You might notice your logical mind assessing, and maybe even objecting to, The Council's messages: *This all sounds too easy (or difficult). This doesn't make sense. I don't get it. There's no way this level of joy and abundance is possible for me.* In these moments, take a few deep breaths and focus on moving your awareness from your head to your heart. It may even help to place your hand on your heart, which will connect you to the deeper aspects of you. The simple act of acknowledging what is so for you in the moment allows new possibilities.

Many masters in The Council here on Earth have realized the power of The Council's teachings through repetition. As such, I encourage you to read and reread this book, time and time again, paying particular attention to the sections that most call to you.

Most of all . . . Enjoy! Have fun! Let this be the magical adventure it is meant to be.

A NOTE FROM THE AUTHOR

As you read the pages of this amazing book, you may notice that The Council frequently repeats their messages and guidance to you. They do this intentionally. Their purpose in doing this is because often our human mind must hear something several times before we actually *"get it."* The wisdom of The Council is of a highly vibrational nature, and repetition is key to ensuring that you absorb the essence of this information.

The Council tells us that first, we must come into the awareness of the information. Once we do, we can have an experience that allows the wisdom to go deeper and become *truth*. As you reread the pages of this book, you will be astounded when you absorb information that you totally missed the first time you read it. The Council's extraordinary divine wisdom is a great gift to you and to all of humanity. *Love and treasure it with all your heart!*

AN OPENING
MESSAGE FROM
THE COUNCIL

We are not separate from you, which is why we are
always available to you. We are always with you
and always available to you.

— THE COUNCIL

We are so pleased and delighted to have the opportunity to
speak with you on this magical and glorious day indeed. While
our words to you are important, this is a vibrational experience,
one of remembering the truth of who you really are, why you are
here, and all that you intended when you chose this magnificent
life experience—because we assure you that your life is meant to
be so very miraculous, magical, and masterful indeed.

There is so much here to explore. There is so much fun to be
had. There are so many opportunities for you to play and create with all of creation while living your greatest potential as the
enlightened, realized, awakened, embodied master that you are.
Remember that you came here, at this time, to live the greatest
expression of all that you are on beloved Mother Earth. That is
how important you are! And as you embody the master that you
are, we assure you that you will create a life beyond your wildest dreams.

Your life is meant to be so very good for you. Your life is meant
to be miraculous. Your life is meant to be magical. Your life is

meant to be the endless expression of your highest creation—an endless, joyful, abundant manifestation.

Throughout the vast history of humanity, there are portals of potential and possibility where whole new realities become possible—where the unseen can manifest to the seen faster than ever before. This is one of those times, and it is a very powerful and important time in your human experience, one where everything is at the highest level of potential, possibility, manifestation, and creation. It is a time of great expansion, and new levels of creation on Earth—a journey to your New Earth reality.

This is your time, dear master. This is your time to shine, to create, and to allow your power. Your divine gifts are for you and all of humanity. Your abilities, your talents, your skills, your hopes, your dreams, your wishes—they are all part of the unique gift that you are in this human incarnation on this beautiful planet at this time. It matters not how you have thought about creation. It matters not how you have held yourself in lack and limitation and separation and fear. It matters not. All that matters now is your awareness, your presence, your consciousness, in this moment. Be *all that you are* and bring all that you are into *this* moment.

You are a heavenly manifestation of Source Energy in physical form. You, dear master, can do anything. You, dear master, can create anything that you wish. You, dear master, can have it all, whatever that means for you. You can have it all—the love, the abundance, the joy, the richness, the beauty, the freedom, the well-being, and the vitality that you desire. And you will just expand from there. You can have it all, and from that state, you will go deeper and deeper into new ways of creating and expressing yourself. You can have it all, and from that place, new experiences and so much more to explore will present themselves to you.

What is it that you *most* wish for in the depths of your heart, in the depths of your being, from the highest levels of your beautiful soul, dear master? What is it that you wish for? Because that wish was placed in your heart by you, for you. That wish was placed in your heart by your soul, by your higher self—the part of you that has never known limitation, that has never known lack, and that has never known separation. This part of you is the truth of you—the part of you that never forgets who you really are, why you are here, and all that you intended when you chose this magnificent life experience.

We remind you, as we often do, dear master, that you are everything you wish to be. You already are. You are both what you know yourself to be and all that you will become through the process of expansion, expression, and new experiences. You are here to create with All That Is—the highest expression of all that you are. You are here to create your masterpiece, your legacy, your dream. You're here to write your story and everything you wish it to be. You're here to live life at the highest levels beyond lack, beyond limitation, beyond fear, beyond separation, beyond doubt, beyond distraction, beyond resistance, beyond reaction.

In every moment, *remember* the power of your consciousness, *remember* the power of your presence, *remember* the love that you are, and *remember* that you are the powerful Creator of your reality. At this time, dear master, it is most important that you shine the light that you are for all to see throughout all of Heaven and Earth. For this is how you will expand upon Heaven and Earth, this is how you will expand upon paradise, this is how you will expand upon the Promised Land, and this is how you will allow the realization of new levels of creation.

The New Earth is here now. As you realize yourself as the powerful Creator of the New Earth, you will go beyond into new potentials and possibilities; you will realize even more beauty, more abundance, more well-being, more love, and more freedom and power to create. And as you allow your awareness and your consciousness into the absolute knowing of all that you are and all you intended for your life experience, you will bring yourself into new levels of power, new levels of creation, new levels of everything. There is only *more*. You will continue to expand this expression of you. You will continue to expand your experiences. You will continue to expand all that is here for you to explore. And in doing so, you are expanding the potentials and possibilities for your beloved human family to realize more of this truth within them too.

You are starting to open to the intelligence all around you by fully opening to and allowing the intelligence that is within you. You are fully opening to the manifestation all around you as you allow yourself to open to the manifestation within you, and to the heavenly manifestation that is you. Let it in, dear master—the love that you are, the power that you are, the light that you are. Allow it, receive it, welcome it, celebrate it, and rejoice in it. It is all here for you now.

We know there are many distractions, moments of resistance and reaction, in your human experience that separate you from paradise, from Heaven on Earth, from the New Earth, when you allow them into your focus. Remember, dear master, that you have the power to choose—to stay conscious, to stay present, and to create your reality the way you want to in every moment. We remind you, with great love for you and with the most tender, gentle kindness: *Nothing* can stop you from experiencing Heaven on Earth, dear master, but you.

Nothing can stop you but the stories you tell yourself about you and about all that you perceive. This is how powerful you are. And dear master, *nothing* is worth your Heaven on Earth. Nothing. Stay in your joy. Stay in peace. Stay in love. Stay in harmony, because these are some of the things you most wish for.

You are never alone, dear master. You were never alone, and you're going to understand more now than ever before how loved you are, how guided you are, how protected you are, and how assisted you are every moment of every day throughout your entire human experience.

There is great love here for you. There is so much love within you and all around you in every moment. As you open to it, as you allow it, as you welcome it, as you receive it, as you celebrate it, it just expands. And that is true with everything. Oh, the magic that is here for you, the abundance that is here for you, the joy that is here for you, the love that is here for you, the freedom that is here for you, the beauty that is here for you, and the well-being that is here for you. *As you embody it, it expands. As you realize it, it expands. As you realize abundance, abundance expands. As you realize joy, joy expands. As you realize love, love expands. As you realize freedom, freedom expands. As you realize beauty, beauty expands. As you realize well-being, well-being expands.*

Your highest well-being is here for you now. An abundant, rich, prosperous life is your divine, inherent birthright. It is not something you force or demand. It is something that you allow through your joy, your creations, your expressions, your expansion. And when you fully allow yourself—*all* that you are—into the process of creation in every moment, the highest expression of you becomes manifest in physical form for you and for all to see.

You are endless. You are eternal. There is nothing, dear master, that could ever happen to your physical body or in your life circumstance that could ever threaten your infinite well-being. Everything is always happening *for* you. Whatever is going on right now in your life is simply an upgrade of your current operating systems. Whatever is going on in your body, in your relationships, in your financials, in your work, is taking you into new levels of health and well-being and creation. As you perceive your experiences this way, new features, new functionalities, new potentials, and new possibilities will become available to you.

There is so much more going on here than your human mind can comprehend. But you are allowing your upgrades! You are allowing the lighter, brighter, happier, more joyful, more peaceful, and more loving energies that are going to help you to thrive in the New Earth.

And, dear master, you are here to create your Heaven on Earth. You are here to create your life the way you wish it to be; you are here to create reality and then experience it with all of your physical senses. You are here to create, but not through the old, limited ways of pushing, forcing, and efforting personal transformation and external manifestations because you don't like who or what you are, and are not where you want to be. No, this is not creation as we speak of it. *True Creation* is what you really want. True

Creation is expanding the potentials and the possibilities by feeling your way into an even greater expression of who you really are.

If you cannot "figure out" how something could be possible for you, remember that it is not your job to figure it out. It's your job to feel your way into these dreams in your heart. Allow the feeling of what you want in this now moment, and in the next, and in the next; welcome it and celebrate it now. Rejoice now in the abundance and wealth and prosperity and richness that is *inherently* yours, and your manifestations will be the highest expressions of these truths.

Let nothing keep you from the dreams in your heart, dear master. Go into your heart, set your dreams free, let them fly, let them soar, let them be free to expand and to draw to you that which is even beyond your wildest dreams come true. Don't let your doubts, your fears, your belief in limitation keep you from the dreams in your heart. You are here to realize yourself as the powerful Creator of your reality. As you think of the Source, the Divine, the Creator, God, Supreme Being, you do not think of lack, you do not think of any limitation, you do not think of separation, you do not think of fear, you do not think of struggle. You think of powerful presence, creation, freedom, abundance, and love. This is who you are.

It is time, dear master, to come into harmony with all of you. Realization is the integration of every part of you—all that is you, all that is within you, and all that is available to you. As you come into harmony with all of you, you come into the powerful force of True Creation that allows anything and everything that is possible for you to be manifested through you.

It is also time to come into harmony with All That Is. Come into harmony with nature—the land, the animals, the plants, the air, and the water. Come into harmony with your beloved human family. Come into harmony with the infinite intelligence all around you. Come into harmony with your soul, your spirit, and your soul family, and come into harmony with the Source, the Heavens, and the stars. As you come into harmony, there is well-being, there is abundance, and there is freedom, love, peace, and inspiration. It is all here for you now.

The greatest dream you could dream for your beloved human family is that of love, joy, peace, abundance, well-being, freedom, beauty, and harmony for all. In this dream, you live in harmony with one another, with nature, with All That Is, and by coming together in the awareness of your oneness there is more of everything for everyone. There is a dream within your heart for this realization to become your reality, but to have this dream manifest, you must realize it first for yourself. As you realize it for yourself, and as you see your dreams come true, you make it possible for all of humankind to do the same.

Embody the love that you are as that which you call God. In this, you are allowing your infinite worth, you are allowing your infinite abundance, you are allowing your infinite well-being, you are allowing your infinite love, and you are allowing the infinite intelligence that has never forgotten who you are or why you are here and all that is possible for you. This is the force that creates worlds; you are the force that creates worlds.

And, dear master, know that all of humankind carries this seed of potential within them. As you become aware of it, those seeds begin to grow. As you shine your light, those seeds begin to sprout and blossom. Soon enough you will have created a beautiful garden, and all will begin to realize the power, the love, and the light within you and within them. This is why you are here. This is why we are here. We came forth because we promised we would.

May you realize the true power within you.
May you realize that you are everything you wish to be.
You already are. It is all within you, and it has always been.
May you know the light that you are.
May you create your masterpiece.

You are us. We are you. And we could not love you more.

We love you. We love you. We love you.

CHAPTER ONE

CELEBRATE YOUR MAGNIFICENT TRANSFORMATION

In this chapter, The Council reminds you to acknowledge your personal transformation and pause to appreciate all that you have become before focusing on the next adventure.

We are so pleased to be here with you at this time in this incredible, incredible, sacred space that you create with your energy, your focus, and your intention to remember who you really are, why you are here, and what you intended when you chose this magnificent life experience. Your life can be everything you wish it to be. You are everything you wish to be. *You already are.*

We know that there's great excitement as you come into this new understanding and a new chapter of your life experience. But what if it's not just a new chapter? What if it's a whole new book? What if it's a whole new *story*? A whole new *reality*? A whole new you, indeed. However, do not for a moment miss the opportunity to celebrate how truly magnificent you are and how truly magnificent this life experience has been for you. Every step of the way led you to the here and now. *Be here now.*

As we feel your excitement to move into new beginnings and new opportunities, we tell you it is *beyond* what you could even imagine asking for. It is beyond what you could even imagine from your viewpoint here in this moment.

Think for a moment. We don't do this often, but from your current place of alignment, from your place of presence, think for a moment back to 10 years ago. Do you even remember who that person was? Think of a picture of yourself from that time frame. Think of what you did around that time. Maybe something significant comes to your mind. *Can you even believe that you are the person that you knew yourself to be a whole decade ago?*

Look who you are now. That person 10 years ago was special and beautiful and loved and magnificent and radiant in their own way, but *look how far you have come.* Could you *ever* have imagined that you would be where you are right now, that you would become the you that you know as you?

**Could you ever have imagined that
you would come this far?**

We know there are things you still desire and experiences you still wish to have. We assure you, it's just beginning to get good for you. Be excited to begin to expand your awareness into where this is all going for you. However, we want you to take a moment to see how far you have come in the past year, in the past month, in the past *week*. Perhaps even in the past couple of days you have shifted into a newer, bigger, more expanded version of all that you are. Approximately 10 years ago in this life that you know, in this time that you participate in, think for a moment. *Wow. How far I have come. It took great courage to come this far.* It's time to celebrate your transformation!

The past 10 years have been a decade of transformation. If you were to get a physical picture of yourself from 10 years ago and put it next to a picture of you in your present, you would see the difference in your eyes. You would see the difference in your energy. You would see the difference in your *aliveness.*

Now, some of you might focus on the age. Some of you might focus on the superficial. But if you really, really tuned in energetically, *wow, you have undergone the most miraculous transformation. You have!* You have transformed, truly. At this time, there's not one single cell in your body that was in your body 10 years ago. Not one single cell. How those cells rejuvenated themselves was based on your beliefs, your intention, your focus, your level of consciousness.

Anything and everything is possible for you, we assure you.

From this moment here, just turn around and look at how far you have come. We think one thing peculiar, and it is this: If you think about it this way, your bodies are designed to perceive what is in front of you, and therefore you are always focused on what's in front of you and where you are going. Your eyes face forward. Some of you have some awareness of your periphery, but for the most part you're focused on going forward.

Why do we find this peculiar? We agree that intention, focus, and desire all create the momentum forward. For most of your life experience, you're focused on what's in front of you and on moving forward. Many of you are eager to jump into the next thing. *Let's get this over with and on to a new beginning,* you think. While we understand, we would tell you that there are fabulous gifts here for you in this time, in this very sacred time between now and you stepping into the next chapter of your life experience.

We urge you—take a moment and turn around. There's a whole world to perceive just by turning around for a moment. In your place of power, in the moment, from a place of presence, just turn around and look how far you have come. Look how much you have *become.*

Have you received all that has been given? Have you *fully* received all that has been given? Have you received all that you have become? Have you *fully* received all that you have become? Have you *really* appreciated all that you have become, all that you have been given, and all that you are? Have you really *realized* the fullness of the transformation that has occurred?

**Pause and appreciate all that you have become, all
that you have been given, and all that you are.**

A transformation has occurred. The past decade of your life
has been about transformation. Transforming your beliefs, transforming your body, transforming your relationships, transforming
your profession and career, and transforming how you relate—but
ultimately transforming *you*.

Every single thing is about *you*, your relationship to all things
in your life. How you relate to others. How you relate to your body.
How you relate based on your belief system. You've gone through
an incredible transformation. Before we jump into what the next
10 years is going to be about for you, take a moment and just turn
around and look at how far you have come.

We will give you a perfect visual to hold in your mind. Imagine that you have just climbed the highest mountain, that you
have just run a marathon, that you have just gone through the
most incredible challenge, whatever it is. What would it be for you
if you were to set up the greatest challenge of your life? Jumping
out of an airplane? Swimming across the ocean? Having the courage to move across the country, to start a new career, or end an
unhealthy relationship? *What would the greatest challenge be for you?*

Imagine that you are just about to cross the proverbial finish line. There, waiting for you with your arms out wide and the
biggest smile on your face is you. It's *you* waiting for you at the
finish line.

You're almost there, just a couple more steps. You can see it
now, and there you are at the finish line. The grandest, most loving, most conscious, beautiful, magnificent version of you is waiting for you. It's your soul. It's your higher self. It's you and all parts
of you. It's you, the bright, beautiful light that is you. The ever-
present, eternal being that you are, the being of light, the being
of consciousness that you are, is waiting for you. You're just about

there, a few more steps. You're going to pass through the barrier and break through. *There you will fall into the arms of you.*

One more step. You're almost there. You're almost in your arms. You're almost there. Go, you can do it. You can do it. You're there. You did it. You did it!

Fall into the arms of you, laughing, crying, relieved, excited. Oh, there are no words. There are no words. You did it. Now embrace yourself, and love yourself, love yourself, love yourself. Look into your eyes, fall into your arms, melt into your heart. You did it. The greatest challenge. The transformation is complete. You did it, and you did a great job. You made it. You're here.

Your incredible transformation is complete.
You did it, and you did a great job.

You made it through a decade of transformation. You're here. How does it feel? You did it, and you're safe in your arms. You're free. You're home. You're home, completely safe and fully free in your home. You did it.

Wow. What an incredible decade this has been. What an incredible challenge. You have made it, and you can now look back at all the practice and all the training and all the preparing for this challenge. Remember the hours you spent, all of the adventures along the way, all of the memories, all of the joy, all of the love, all of the wisdom, all that you gained on the journey.

Keep your heart open, keep your awareness open, and allow yourself to *really* see how far you have come. Look at *all* that has transformed, but look at you, the absolute most magnificent manifestation of transformation. You are the manifestation of transformation.

**Keep your heart and your awareness open.
Look at the magnificent manifestation of
transformation that you are.**

———

Take this time to appreciate. Take this time to be grateful. Take this time to really receive all that you have been given. Take this time to really receive all that you have become.

We know you're excited for what's coming. We too are excited for what's coming, but don't forget who you have become. A decade of transformation is almost complete, but the final step of transformation . . . if you think about it, you know what it is. What is it? What is the final step of transformation?

In the most perfect metaphorical example, the butterfly starts as a caterpillar crawling on the ground. It only understands life from the viewpoint of crawling on the ground. It can only see as vastly as it can see what's in front of it from the perspective of crawling on the ground. Then it builds itself a cocoon. It doesn't really know what it's doing. It's just being guided somehow. There's some intelligence that inspires a caterpillar to build a cocoon. It doesn't really know what it's doing and certainly wouldn't know how to answer the question, if asked, "What are you doing, caterpillar?" It doesn't know. It's just doing what it can't help but do. There's just something moving it, guiding it to create a cocoon and go within. It doesn't yet know that it's transforming.

Over time, as you look from the outside, you might not think that much is happening until the day that the cocoon begins to open, and you can see that there's something there. It's different. Something has changed. It may take some time for the butterfly to realize it's no longer a caterpillar crawling on the ground, but then it remembers. It knows who it was and who it is now, and it knows what it is now capable of. It looks up at the sky.

The final step of transformation is when the butterfly spreads out its wings and decides to fly. The butterfly takes off from the cocoon and begins a whole new story, a whole new life, a whole new reality. There's so much more this beautiful butterfly, flapping its wings and flying high, can experience. There's so much more to enjoy. It gets where it wants to go with an effortless ease because it's no longer crawling on the ground. Now, it soars.

———

**The final step of transformation is to fly.
And it's your time.**

———

You are all butterflies. Some of you are still in the cocoon just about to remember who you really are, just about to recognize yourself as a butterfly with wings. Some of you have already discovered that you have wings, and some of you have remembered that the wings will help you fly. Some of you already are standing at the edge of the cocoon, and you're just about to flap your wings for the first time and really lift off. Some of you have lifted off, and you've taken that first moment of flight.

Oh, it's so good. You almost don't want to rush that first moment of flight. But when you flap your wings for the first time, and you take off and fly—*oh, isn't it the most magnificent feeling?* There, in that moment, you realize you can do anything, you can have anything, you can go anywhere. Anything and everything is possible for you because now you can fly.

That butterfly flying in the sky, in perfect harmony with nature, flying high for all the world to see, is you. You are free. *You are free.*

Allow the transformation to come full circle. There's no end. And there's really no beginning. You are just allowing the transformation to come full circle. If you were to go back once you've seen the butterfly and try to find the caterpillar somewhere within it, you would realize it's simply no longer there. There's something more beautiful and magical in its place. You wouldn't worry about where it went or how it happened. You would just admire the beauty of all that the caterpillar has become. It's time to really admire *all that you have become.*

Yes, there's a new story emerging. Yes, there is a new book to be written here. There's a new story to tell. *Everything really is always getting better.* The best is *always* unfolding for you, in every single moment. But for now, pause. Take this time to spread your wings and fly and feel what it's like to be transformed.

———

There are new adventures. Everything really is always getting better. The best is always unfolding for you in every moment.

———

Oh, it's beautiful. You're beautiful. This life is beautiful. This journey is beautiful. You are everything you wish to be. Now you know who you are. Every moment to come will reveal a new opportunity, a new adventure, a time to live, to love, to fully be all that you are. A time to experience self-realization at its *fullest.*

And it just gets better. You are stepping into the decade of the master, the fully self-realized master that you are, and what it's like to be a living master of your life experience. Oh, there's so much yet to come!

We are *so* excited about your life, about your experiences, but take the time to really realize what an incredible transformation has occurred, the transformation of *you* into being all that you are. *Oh, and fly. And fly.* Take that step, flap your wings, and let go. Let go. Go with the wind. Let the air and your wings take you higher.

We love you so, so very much. We could not be more excited about your life. We could not, truly. How far you have come on your journey is truly remarkable. You are *celebrated.* You are *honored.* You are *loved.* You are so supported from our side. *Be all that you are.* Be all that you are.

ESSENTIAL MESSAGES

- Look who you are now. That person 10 years ago was special and beautiful and loved and magnificent and radiant in their own way, but *look how far you have come.*

- Pause and appreciate all that you have become, all that you have been given, and all that you are.

- Do not for a moment miss the opportunity to celebrate how truly magnificent you are and how truly magnificent this life experience has been for you. Every step of the way led you here, now.

- At this time, there's not one single cell in your body that was in your body 10 years ago. Not one single cell. How those cells rejuvenated themselves was based on your beliefs, your intention, your focus, your level of consciousness.

- Keep your heart open, keep your awareness open, and allow yourself in this time to *really* see how far you have come. Look at *all* that has transformed, but look inside, look at you, the absolute most magnificent manifestation of transformation.

- The best is always unfolding for you in every moment but take this time to spread your wings, fly, and feel what it's like to be transformed.

- Keep your heart and your awareness open. Look at the magnificent manifestation of transformation that you are.

CHAPTER TWO

I Am the Master, I Am the Magic, I Am the Miracle

**In this chapter, The Council assures you that nothing is
stopping you from creating the life you wish to live, and you
cannot even fathom the magic you are expanding into.**

We are so pleased and delighted to have the opportunity to
be here with you all. It is time for you to invite in all of the magic
that is here for you in your life. Your lives are meant to be magical.
What better time than now to ride the rockets of magical energy
that are here for you?

What is magic? It's the absolute power of you opening and
allowing your energy, opening and allowing yourself to be the
miracle in the world, opening and allowing yourself to be all that
you are and to experience all that is here for you. There is nothing better than fully living your life, fully loving yourself, and
allowing magic to present itself to you in your life experience. Not
from a place of specific expectation of what you want to see happen, but from a place of opening and allowing magic to surprise,
delight, and excite you. It's time to get really, really excited about
your lives.

You are heading into an incredible time in your experience,
a time to focus clearly on the energy that you are made of, to
see clearly this game of life that you are playing, to understand
your perspective, knowing that *consciousness is where it's at*. It is

all about consciousness. You are spiritual beings having a human experience, but beyond that you are beginning to know yourself as the *consciousness* that you are. That consciousness is ever present. It is eternal. It is always expanding and becoming more, yet needs nothing, wants for nothing. The energy is drawn to your consciousness.

Your consciousness attracts energy. It attracts light. It attracts flow and power and magic and miracles. It attracts divine orchestration. It attracts energy to come in and serve you. The more you know your consciousness and how it has the power to draw energy, to draw magic, to draw miracles to you, and to divinely orchestrate all things for you, the more you will focus yourself into the consciousness that you are, into all that you are, and you will begin to know yourself as the Creator. Allow yourself to flow easily through this time as you step more fully into knowing yourself as the Creator of your life experience.

What are you creating? There is *nothing* stopping you. We assure you there is nothing stopping you. Health, wealth, abundance, well-being, love, relationships, *anything!* There is nothing stopping you. Whatever *may* have been stopping you in the past is not stopping you now.

———

What are you creating?
There is nothing stopping you.

———

You have elevated yourself beyond a consciousness of victimhood, of powerlessness. You are elevating yourself beyond a consciousness of feeling stuck or struggling or in lack or broken in any way. You are elevating yourself to be the I Am Creator energy that is you when you fully allow your consciousness. *What are you creating?* Because in every moment you *are*. It is beyond even knowing yourself as manifestation. It is knowing yourself as the Creator. Can you allow yourself to be the Creator of your life experience?

We often say to move out of the doing and into the being and allow things to come with effortless ease, to allow things to unfold for you in the most miraculous ways. Indeed, that is the basis of our message, but to know yourself as the Creator, to know yourself as the energy that creates, to understand that *you already are manifestation* is different. You're here in form, which means you already are manifestation. Every moment, you are the living expression of manifestation, but you will begin manifesting from a state of *consciousness*, rather than from a state of lack or not-enoughness.

There is a difference. There is a deeper understanding here for you if you're ready for it, and if you're ready to hear it. Nothing's stopping you. Nothing's holding you back. *You can have it all right here, right now.* Yes, there are things that will unfold. Yes, you are drawing things to you from your force field, but in knowing the consciousness that you *are*, you do not need or want for anything. Creation comes from a place of wholeness and pureness, and manifestation then comes as a reflection of your wholeness, your completeness, and your mastery. Whatever is, is here through your consciousness. That is truly a *wonderful* thing.

You, as the master, begin to know that you create what you want to experience, and that you create for you and only you. It doesn't matter who or what or when the manifestation shows up because you're creating for you and only you.

A great majority of your manifestations or your desire for manifestation, what you want and what you need—or think you need—is based on others showing up to do it for you or with you or to help you or support you. That's a wonderful thing, but again, there's a difference between creating from a place of wholeness and wanting to manifest something because you think having it will satisfy your needing and your wanting.

You have the power to satiate yourself in this moment, not just satisfy a need or a want, but to fully delight in all that is here for you. Your consciousness is what will ignite your soul. Your consciousness is what will excite you and delight you, and it will guide you to knowing that you are the Creator.

You have the power to fully satiate yourself in every moment and delight in all that is here for you. Your consciousness is what will ignite your soul.

You're ready to go deeper. You're ready for more. You're ready to hear it. There is so much love encased in the words we are telling you, in the energy that we bring forth to you. There is so much love here for you. There is *only* love here for you. We come forth only because we know your deepest intention is to live your life fully and to love yourself fully and to be all that you are. In living your highest expression, you will illuminate the potential for your beloved human family to open and allow the energy that is here for them, to open and allow magic and miracles in their *own* experience.

Be all that you are from the energy of the powerful Creator that is you. *What are you creating?* The answer to that might be very different than what you said in the past when someone asked the question, *what do you want?*

There are levels of consciousness, there are levels of mastery, there are levels of manifestation, and there are levels of truth, but none is more important or better than the other. As you begin to elevate your consciousness, you move into different layers of experience and potential.

How good does it feel to know that you are illuminating the potential for humanity? How good does it feel to know that you are illuminating the potential for another? How good does it feel to stand in your power, to stand in your light, to be all that you are? How good does it feel to open and expand your consciousness and invite in greater, deeper, more meaningful experiences? Not because you weren't enough or lacked for anything, but for the pure joy and delight of living more fully and allowing your consciousness to fully express yourself, and to experience all that is here for you. We assure you, you still can't even *fathom* the absolute magical, miraculous life that you are expanding into.

What are you creating? Because nothing is stopping you. Nothing is in your way. Love, health, wealth, all of it, all of it. As you begin to take responsibility for what you are creating, say it out loud. Recognize your work. "I am creating a wonderful day. I am creating an abundant day. I am creating an abundant week. I am creating an abundant month."

What are your intentions for this time? We come forth to offer you our messages, our awareness of where you are and what is coming for you, but *what are you creating in this day, in this week, in this month, in this time?*

What if—just *what if*—this was your last month in the life experience you know as you? What if this was the final chapter of *this* story that you've been telling in the place that you are, with the people you're with, the family that you know in this experience? What if? Would that give you permission to set yourself free, to be all that you are? Would *that* give you permission to love fully and to love yourself fully? Would that give you permission to *finally* set yourself free and just *love* and just *be* and just *live*?

Would you put twenty-dollar bills or five-dollar bills in your pocket and give them freely? Would you finally find all the magnificent things to appreciate about your body? Would you give your family a break and let them be who they are, where they are, and love them the way they are and as who they have been to you? Would you accept your friends as they are, not needing them to change or be any different? Would the doorman or the person that checks out your groceries seem just a little more divine in your eyes?

Would you be a little kinder and a little more generous? A little more open and a little more loving? If this were the last month as you, in this experience here and now, *could you finally set yourself free?* If in this last month you really, really could be who you want to be, have what you want to have, and do what you want to do— and experience it to the *absolute fullest*—it might make everything so incredibly simple. Each day would be sacred, each moment a gift, and every experience an opportunity to love. Each day would be an invitation to live more fully and to allow miracles to flow through you, to allow yourself to *be* a miracle.

Would that not be magical? *Magical.* You can decide, and you can choose. You can choose. *I am creating a magical day. I am creating a magical week. I am creating a magical month. I am creating a magical life. I am the magic, the unexplainable, unforeseen, unfolding of the Divine. I am the unfathomable, unforeseen, unexplainable expression of love in the world.*

Allow yourself to be the magic. You *are.* You are the magic, and you are the miracle because you are the master. There is nothing stopping you. There is *nothing* in your way.

Can you allow yourself the freedom to be the miracle, to be the magic, to be the master of your existence? All it takes is setting yourself free—but freedom requires responsibility. Freedom requires *total* responsibility for *your* energy. Not taking energy from others. Not blaming others for your energy. Not feeding off others' energy. No, take total responsibility for your energy. *Total responsibility for where your consciousness is.* Total responsibility will give you freedom.

We know you really don't intend to take energy from others. You don't intend to feed off others' energies. You don't intend to blame others for your energy. It's just a habit from when you didn't understand your power. It's as *simple* as when you used training wheels because you hadn't yet mastered how to ride the bike. It's not that big of a deal. When you figure out how to ride the bike, you take the training wheels off. When you figure out your energy and how to allow it, you take total responsibility. Taking the training wheels off the bike is total responsibility for you, as the one riding the bike, deciding where it's going to go and how fast it's going to go, and if it is going to go up the hill or down the hill. Total responsibility for *your* energy, for *your* consciousness. Because *truly,* consciousness is everything.

But how does one move into being ready to embrace a higher consciousness? How your beliefs tend to evolve in the human experience often begins with a journey of exploring religion and what it has to offer you, exploring prayer and ritual and ceremony and scripture and practices, and even exploring shared experiences with like-minded people. Some of you had parents who were very, very religious. Some of you had parents who were not very religious. But there was curiosity around questions such as: *What is God? What is religion's relationship with God? How does religion relate to God?* You explored how religion related to God and how God related to religion.

Then you began to explore spirituality, what you might call the New Age or metaphysics. It expanded your awareness of what you thought God was. Now it included angels, it included spirit guides, it included your soul within the concept of God. Sometimes you got your energy from these things. Perhaps you believed that the angels were flowing energy to you, and that made you feel better. You explored the relationship between spirituality and God and all things that that meant for you—angels, guides, your higher self, your soul—all in relation to this concept of God and the Creator. *Who was creating it all, and where was the energy coming from? Where was the all-knowing mind, and where were the answers? Were they in the Akashic records? Where were they?* You knew the energy of all things that you considered sacred was available to you and you chose to bring it into your life in all of these various forms.

Now you're ready to move into consciousness, because achieving consciousness means you are moving only to where energy serves you. You are accessing freedom and becoming the Creator of your life. We go back to saying freedom requires responsibility, *total responsibility* for your energy. Not blaming or feeding off any other energy. You will begin to know *yourself* as the Creator, as consciousness, even to know that all of it is within you, that *you* are that which you call God. Angels and guides and your higher self and all gods are an extension of your own consciousness. They are an extension of *your own* consciousness, which means you have total freedom. The energy that creates worlds is always available to you when you open and allow your energy to serve you, when you become conscious of yourself as free, as the Creator.

You are that which you call God.

———

Consciousness is everything, period. Consciousness is what creates, and consciousness is what attracts energy. Consciousness is love. The more conscious you are, the more loving you are. The more conscious you are, the more open you are. The more conscious you are, the more forgiving you are. The more conscious you are, the more generous you are.

The healthier you are, the more abundant you are, the more loving you are, the more conscious you are. That's not to say that people can't be healthy and be unconscious. That's not to say that people can't be in love and be unconscious. There's some level of consciousness there, but we are talking to you about a much deeper understanding of consciousness and of you as the Creator opening and allowing your energy.

As you are moving from spirituality into consciousness, knowing that all things are an extension of you, you begin to really know yourself as capable of mastering your life. You have the power to take your seat at the Ascended Master table at any moment that you choose. You are that and so much more, but for now, you are here in this life experience. But know that it is all here for you, all accessible to you. Your journey through consciousness is opening any and every potential and possibility for you.

There's some part of you that knows that you're really getting this, that you can really feel it. Even if you can't explain it or articulate it, you're getting it. You can feel it. You can feel it expanding. You can feel the master within you. You can feel all the consciousness is an extension of you. You can feel what it feels like to open and allow your energy. You're starting to *really* get what receiving is all about. You're standing in your power, saying, "Show me. Show me. Show me the magic. Use me for the magic. I am the magic because I am the master. I am the magic because I am the master. I am the miracle. I am the magic. I am the master." That is what you are. And so it is.

How would you live your life more fully in this day, in this week, in this month, at the closing chapter of life as you knew it, as you enter total clarity, total focus, total freedom, total surrender? How would you *be* different in this time if you knew? Because you know now. Feel it as we express these words. Say it with us. "I am the miracle. I am the master. I am the magic. I am the miracle. I am the magic. I am the master. I am the master. I am the magic. I am the miracle." And so it is.

———

I am the master. I am the magic. I am the miracle.

———

You are. You are. You are everything you wish to be. You already are. What are you creating? What is the life you are creating, in the full and total knowing that you are the Creator, that you are creating your life experience?

Consider what you are creating without going into the *doing*, without trying to figure it out, because all of that comes from the scarcity mindset, the sense of lacking something. All of that is coming from a place of lack, because if you needed to figure it out, it would mean that you're lacking something that you need or want. If you're trying to force it and make it happen, it's because what has manifested isn't what you want or need, which would automatically move you into a state of not-enoughness, of separation, instead of into full alignment with yourself as the Creator and your *oneness* with all that you are and all the extensions of consciousness that are you.

That is what oneness means. Oneness doesn't mean that you all come together and do the same things and want the same things and act the same way. That's not what oneness means. *You never needed it to be that way because you knew you were the master of your own life experience.* Yes, you understood that you are all consciousness, that you are all light and vibration. You knew that, but you knew everyone else was also the master. If they chose poverty, it didn't mean you had to. If they chose to live in someplace you didn't want to live, it didn't mean that you had to live there. If they chose to be unkind to themselves, it didn't mean that you had to be unkind to yourself.

You're really getting this. You're really getting this. You have *total* freedom. But in that, you have total responsibility for you and your life and what you create. That is oneness. Oneness is to come into full and total alignment with all that *you* are, which is consciousness. Full and total alignment to the consciousness that you are because consciousness attracts energy. Consciousness is everything. *Consciousness is what creates.*

When you move through the different layers of understanding yourself as the Creator, you go beyond looking at your experience and saying, *what do I want?* You recognize on some level when you're looking at what is and the conditions that have manifested that you *are* somehow responsible for the manifestation of what is in your experience now. When you know that, you know that somehow you have influence over your conditions. You might not know *how*, but you know on some level you have some influence over your conditions. When you reach the point of understanding that influence on every level, you will never want for or need for anything.

You often look at what it is, and you look at what is missing, what's wrong, what's not whole, what's not complete. *What's separate here from me? If I had that thing now that's separate from me, then I would be happy here and now. I would be joyful here and now. I'd be free here and now. I'd be whole. I'd be complete. I'd be worthy. I'd be enough.* From that perspective of *not* being aligned with your wholeness and your oneness with All That Is, you start trying to figure out how you're going to go about getting that thing. That's how you've figured things out. Forced it, chased after it, ran after it, tried to control it, manipulated all circumstances to get what you wanted. There's nothing wrong with that, and there's no judgment from our side ever.

Your consciousness is far beyond all of that now. Your awareness has expanded to such a deeper understanding of how to create. You can stand in your moment, in your power, in your wholeness, in your fullness, with full and total responsibility for what is, total acceptance of what is, because you know it's all perfect. Then nothing's stopping you and nothing's in your way and nothing could ever hold you back.

You stand in your power, in your knowing of yourself as the Creator, as the master, and you merely expand from *here*. You move deeper into expression from *here*. You move deeper into experience from *here*, in your wholeness, in your completeness, in your knowing that all things are an extension *of you*. Then you merely align with it. You merely open and allow. You align with it.

———

You don't get what you want. You get what you are.

———

The difference between that and what many mean by *manifesting* is that to manifest what you want implies that you don't have it. But if you are in the place of the Creator, you know you already have it all and you receive what you *are*, what's aligned to you from your state of wholeness and completeness—the state where you are fully loving, fully being, fully living.

We understand there are specific desires in your heart, but don't create the gap or the separation. *Be here now.* When you're in an experience of lack or separation and you're not in your oneness, that creates the gaps in your experience of well-being, abundance, and joy. *It can be no other way.* When you're in your wholeness, your fullness, your completeness, you know all that you are. When you understand fully *I am the miracle, I am the magic, I am the master,* and you take *that* out in the world, you draw so much to you. Not because you need it or you want it, because you *are* it.

Your interactions with others are so different from this place. You *know* that you are the miracle in the world. You *know* that the magic is you, and you take that with you into all your experiences.

Then your body reflects that to you. Then your abundance reflects that to you. Then your relationships reflect that to you. Everything that you relate with reflects your wholeness, your completeness, your oneness, your *perfection*. In that, you can love your life again. You can love the world again, you can love humanity the way you intended to. You can live and love and be in this experience knowing you are everything you wish to be. You already are.

This time is so magnificent! Say to yourself, "I am the miracle, I am the magic, I am the master—and so it is," and watch your life experience unfold. Watch your magnificence be reflected back to you in all that you are and be present in knowing that this is indeed an important time, an exciting time, a wonderful time.

What if, just *what if*, this were the final chapter of this magnificent story you've been telling? Would it be a happily ever after? Would it be legendary? Would you be a legacy? Would you illuminate the potential in others, in the world? It is your *happily ever after forevermore*.

———

This is your happily ever after forevermore.

———

We have so much love for you. We know our message is strong, but we love you, we love you, we love you. We know the truth of all that you are. We see you in your perfection *always*.

ESSENTIAL MESSAGES

- You are the Creator within your own creation of reality.

- There is nothing better than fully living your life, fully loving yourself, and allowing magic to present itself to you in your life experience all of the time.

- In knowing the consciousness that you *are*, you do not need or want for anything. Creation comes from a place of wholeness and pureness.

- Your consciousness is what will ignite your soul. Your consciousness is what will excite you and delight you.

- Freedom requires *total* responsibility for *your* energy. Not taking energy from others. Not blaming others for your energy. Not feeding off others' energy. *Total responsibility for where your consciousness is.*

- Oneness is to come into full and total alignment with all that you are, which is consciousness.

- You don't get what you think you want. You get more of what you *are*.

- Allow yourself to be the magic. There is nothing stopping you. There is *nothing* in your way.

CHAPTER THREE

STEP INTO THE I AM CREATOR FREQUENCY

In this chapter, The Council welcomes you into a new experience where you can perceive your absolute perfection in every moment, being totally satiated as you live and love fully.

We are so pleased and delighted to have the opportunity to welcome you into a new experience of you, a new you. Not because the prior versions of you were not magnificent—they were indeed—but a new you who knows who you really are and delights and marvels in more deeply discovering all that is here for you. *You have bridged Heaven and Earth to create a reality where you have truly remembered that Heaven on Earth is here for you.*

How would you like to live in Heaven on Earth? How do you like to love in Heaven on Earth? How would you like to play in Heaven on Earth? How do you like to create in Heaven on Earth?

You know how to create through force and effort. You know what it's like to struggle and sacrifice. You know what it feels like to experience lack, limitation, fear, and separation. So now ask yourself, *What does my experience look like in Heaven on Earth?*

What does your experience look like in Heaven on Earth?

That is what is here for you now. A new you, a decade of mastery where you fully live in Heaven on Earth. It is in the palm of your hands. Before you is the kingdom. Within you is the kingdom. All around you is the kingdom. Heaven on Earth is here for you, and it is here for you now.

We're going to express something a little differently than we ever have before because we want you to understand what Heaven on Earth is. Heaven on Earth is a new state of consciousness. We also call it the New Earth as it is a new consciousness. It is you allowing yourself to step into elevated, expanded levels of consciousness and beginning to bring through you an expanded perspective of what's possible in your human experience.

Heaven on Earth is a perception. It's a way of perceiving in this experience. You are remembering how to create your reality without having to create an experience of lack in order to move it into form.

———

Heaven on Earth—the New Earth—is an elevated state of consciousness. It is an expanded way of perceiving. And you can access it.

———

Consciousness, as we have said, is everything. Now you're going to really understand *why.* Because that's what creates the magic. That's what creates the miracles. That's what creates the potentials and possibilities. That's what creates your life and your reality to be everything you wish it to be.

Yet you may be realizing that it is in being here now, in your Heaven on Earth, that *you do not desire to be anywhere else but here, now.* You don't need anything, and you don't want anything, because you know from the level of consciousness that you are in that you truly do have it all. You do.

Indeed, the next 10 years of time and space as you experience them will not be about transformation in the way the past 10 years have been. It's not about fixing yourself. It's not about getting what you don't have. It's not about trying to transform the unwanted into the wanted. You have had that type of transformation, where you experienced lack and created what fullness would be after having explored limitation. You explored suffering. You explored worry and stress. You also explored how it took a lot of effort and momentum and action to move things into form.

That transformation has occurred. There's no longer anything to wait for. You're not waiting for anyone else or for some big event in the ethers to facilitate your transformation. You are transformed because you're here now.

Now it is time to play and create in a new level of consciousness. You can play, you can enjoy, because you are where you need to be. You have the power to create because you are the Creator. This is your decade of mastery and magic and miracles and understanding how to create your reality without having to drag it into density and lack and limitation, or having to create a gap between where you are and what you want. You're moving beyond polarity into pure bliss and beauty and feeling totally satiated in every moment of your life experience.

———

The transformation has occurred. There's nothing to wait for. Now is the time to play and create in new levels of consciousness.

———

There's nothing to fix because there's nothing wrong with you. You're not broken. There's nothing more to do. *It's all done. It's all here.* It's about receiving all that is here for you, all that you have become, and not just celebrating who you are on one day of the year, and not just celebrating life on special occasions, but celebrating *every day* and marveling in the magic that is all around you all the time. *It is.* It truly is.

As you move into this new experience, we want to talk to you about setting intentions or making resolutions and how we would look at it a little differently. You probably are looking at it a little differently yourself. Making a resolution would mean that something's wrong with you or that you're not doing something right. You may move into judgment of what you're doing wrong or what you need to do better, and that would not feel very good to you. Even setting goals for a specific time frame probably feels a bit archaic, like something you did in your earlier years, because you have reached a level of spiritual maturity, a level of consciousness, a level of awareness where you don't need to create a gap—of where I am and what I need, and comparing that to who you wish to be—in order to experience *more* of something. You don't need to find something wrong with you to continue to expand and evolve and become all that you are. You are where you are, and you can expand into who you will become with joy and ease.

It is a shift. It's a different way of perceiving, and we really want you to understand what this means. We really want you to understand how perception creates your reality. If you start to perceive your *absolute perfection* in every moment and allow yourself to be totally satiated because you know your own perfection, then there's no lack of anything—ever. You'll find that reality moves through you, that you're the one directing reality—your own reality. As you perceive life from a more expanded, elevated state of consciousness, you begin to fully realize yourself as the Creator of your life experience.

You are the Creator of your life experience, and everything in your reality is an extension of you. All That Is is an extension of you. When you begin to realize yourself as the Creator that you are, you remember what the frequency of I Am Creator feels like in form.

You're here in the human experience. You're here in a plane of form to play in form. You can play in density or you can play in Heaven on Earth. You can dance with creation or to challenge yourself, you can navigate through the murky waters on your own. Either way, you're going to get there. You're going to remember who you really are. You're going to know. You're going to know the Creator that you are of your life experience, so there's nothing wrong with the little challenges that you create for yourself. They all just lead you back to you. They all just help you remember your power. They help you get clear on what you want *more* of, but you no longer need to explore the unwanted with experiences of lack or suffering or struggle to create more of what you already are.

When you truly realize who you are in your essence, then it's just a beautiful dance with creation, and you can play in Heaven on Earth because you know your reality is a result of your perception—how you're perceiving. When you are perceiving life through an expanded, elevated state of consciousness, then every experience will feel like Heaven on Earth. Your experience of life will be one where you are fully living, fully loving, *totally satiated.*

Because many in this time are focused on potential, it's a magical time in your collective consciousness where you can more easily take quantum leaps in shifting your perspective, expanding your awareness, and elevating your consciousness to a whole new level. What you're going for is experiencing the I Am Creator frequency more often throughout the day. The space that doing so creates in your life—the beauty, the joy, the bliss, the ease, the abundance, the richness, the riches, the love (oh, the love), the harmony, the collaboration—is magnificent. It's *magnificent.*

While we recognize that many set goals and many make resolutions during times of change or turmoil or dissatisfaction or even growth, we would invite you to go into the most expanded version of you, the greatest version of you, and feel into that. Live the way you would live if you *already were* the greatest version of you. The only thing that stands between you and you being the greatest version of you, the Creator that you are of your life experience, is your belief in your own worthiness. Believe that you really are worthy, that you really are good enough, that there really isn't anything wrong with you. There really isn't anything to fix. There isn't. There's nothing wrong with you, and there's nothing to fix. You never were broken. You never were. So, let it go. Let it go.

———

The only thing that stands between you and you being the greatest version of you is your belief in your own worthiness.

———

The journey through the transformation time has come and gone. Be here now, be the greatest version of all that you are here and now and remember that you're *free*. You're free from the memories of the past. You're free from the events of your past, of what's happened to you, for you. You're free from the stories. You're free from your belief in not being good enough. You're free from your guilt. You're free from the shame. *You're free from all those things that you explored on your journey to here and now.* Are you really ready in this new day, in this new-you energy, in this new-you frequency, in this new-you consciousness to set yourself free and come home to the truth within?

Some ask why it is that you don't remember your past lives. We tell you, with great love for you, because it's just not that big of a deal. Why would you remember them? You gained all that served you in every experience. You expanded your awareness. You expanded your consciousness. You grew and evolved through all of it. It's just not that big of a deal. The same is true with everything in *this* life experience. Let it go. It's a new day. It's a new time. This is the new you. Let it all go.

Catch yourself when you go into the story, catch yourself when you go into guilt, catch yourself when you go into shame, because what you're doing is turning around and running out of the gate. You're running out of the gate. *You're standing in Heaven on Earth, and you are turning, and you're running out of the gate.* You're running back into the darkness, into the density, into the shame, into the guilt, into the old, into limitation, and you find yourself in a dark, lonely place that you don't want to be anymore.

Let it go. It's not that big of a deal. It's a whole new you here and now. You can transcend everything in this life, and choose to be the living, loving, breathing being that you *are. That you are.*

As you shift your awareness or your perception to understanding that Heaven on Earth is a new consciousness, New Earth is a new consciousness, this time is a new consciousness, the next decade is a new consciousness, the new you is a new consciousness—this is really important—understand that whatever you are holding in *your* consciousness is contributing to *human* consciousness. It's contributing to *global* consciousness. As you expand your con-sciousness into the higher potentials and the grander possibilities of what's truly possible for you here, you infuse *that* into human consciousness.

———

As you expand your consciousness to what's really possible, you infuse that into human consciousness.

———

Understand this. *This is why you're in form.* This is why you're in a body. This is why you came into this human experience. We've said that we're here to help you remember who you are, why you are here, and what you intended. *What you intended was to come into form and expand human consciousness through your own consciousness of what's possible.* It takes someone in form access-ing higher consciousness to begin to move those higher potentials and possibilities into the human experience. *That's the New Earth.* That's what Heaven on Earth is. That's what it means. That's why you're so important.

We are bringing in a whole new awareness and perspective of your life experience. We are expanding upon your purpose, your divine plan. There's more. There's much, much more. The more of you who integrate this within the collective that is all of you, the more you all will expand your consciousness. The awareness that is here will evolve and move into your experience. All of that leads to grander potentials, greater possibilities, a way of living and loving and being in a New Earth, in Heaven on Earth, in *this* life experience.

As you fully remember how important your consciousness is, you begin to see why you went through the transformation you went through and why it's here and now that you're ready to really understand it more and expand your awareness and your con-sciousness. Because if you knew how free you were at certain times in your experience, you would have gone into a hellish experi-ence, blaming yourself, shaming yourself, feeling guilty, getting stuck in the muck, in the mud. You determine your reality with every choice you make, because your reality is merely an extension of you and your perception.

On the other side of the transformation, you can look back and realize that all is forgiven, you are forgiven, there's only love. When you know better, you do better. As you elevate your consciousness, you move through this life experience with ease and grace and love, and you begin to be impeccable with the reality you're creating.

We are going to expand on this because, for example, to set a goal means that you move into density and the sensation of lack, of scarcity. You create the gap in this moment, and you manifest in density until you remember how to create your reality from your alignment to the I Am Creator frequency which is *always* available to you.

Some have asked, *Is there destiny in what's coming? If I don't set a bunch of goals, if I don't make a big plan, maybe I won't get anywhere. Maybe I will just sort of hover around where I am.* We assure you that is not the case. When you are really in the I Am Creator frequency, everything comes to you, everything's clear, everything's easy. It is.

Yes, there are things moving and changing and transforming. There are new realities that you're going to step into living, more expanded realities, more beautiful realities, more loving realities, more abundant realities. There are. You're going to learn how to live in the I Am Creator frequency, creating more of what you are without needing to drag your creations into density for you to *fully* experience living them.

This is part of being impeccable. You can live within any chosen reality you desire to experience without moving it into density, without creating the lack of it, without having to push against the unwanted to align with *more* of what you already *are*.

You can live within any chosen reality you desire to experience without having to push against the unwanted to align with more of what you already are.

Being impeccable is part of a grander conversation we're going to have as you move into the decade of living as the master that you are of your life experience, truly understanding how you and the universe and All That Is work together. Because, as we've said, All That Is is an extension of you. You are an extension of the Source. The Source is an extension of you. You are an aspect of the Divine. The Divine is an aspect of you. You are that which you call God, and God is in everything. So, of course, you create your own reality. What you're really asking for is how to do that with ease and grace in the most magical, miraculous, magnificent ways—how to really remember what it's like to play in Heaven on Earth and dance with all of creation here now.

That's Heaven on Earth. That's the New Earth. That's the state of consciousness that is the new you, that is this new time, that is your next decade.

If you are to set any goal or make any intention, let it be to be fully satiated more of the time. Let it be to feel the I Am Creator frequency in every cell of your body more of the time. Let it be to feel yourself dancing with creation more of the time. But more than anything, let it be here and now in the space *around you* and in the space *within you*. In the space within you, you are perceiving the reality of being totally satiated. You're perceiving the reality of being free to fully live any and every experience that is possible for you. Here and now, in this sacred space, you are *being* the miracle, *being* the magic, *being* the light of the world that you are. In that, you will draw your destiny *to* you, and the divine plan will unfold *through* you.

It's not something you chase after. It's not something you pursue. It's not something you figure out. You draw it to you. The future comes to you. You can create in such an impeccable way that you move yourself into the reality you choose through your perception, and the experience unfolds with ease and certainty and clarity. There's no asking. There's no wondering. There's no trying to figure it out. It's here, and it's now, and it's you.

That is where you are going. That is the new you, a new time, the New Earth, Heaven on Earth.

How would you *live* in Heaven on Earth? How would you *love* in Heaven on Earth? How would you *play* in Heaven on Earth? How would you *create* in Heaven on Earth? Those are the questions. It is here for you now. Feel for the knowing within you, and you will know yourself as the Creator of your life experience. You will recognize the absolute limitless potential that exists within you, the endless possibilities that await you, and the understanding that you are everything you wish to be. You already are the person you wish to be.

We celebrate you. We celebrate you here and now. We celebrate how far you have come. We celebrate where you are going. We celebrate you *coming home*. This is a celebration of you coming home to you. Welcome home. Welcome home. Welcome home. We love you. We love you. We love you.

Take a deep breath. Let it in. Take a deep breath. Let it in. Take a deep breath. Let it in. And so it is.

ESSENTIAL MESSAGES

- Heaven on Earth is a perception. It's an elevated way of perceiving in this human experience.

- You have reached a level of spiritual maturity, a level of consciousness, a level of awareness where you don't need to create the gap between who you wish to be and who you are in order to experience something you want.

- The only thing that stands between you and you being the greatest version of you is your belief in your own worthiness.

- If you are to set any goal or make any intention, let it be to be fully satiated more of the time, to feel the I Am Creator frequency in every cell of your body more of the time, and to feel yourself dancing with creation more of the time.

- When you begin to realize yourself as the Creator that you are, you remember what the frequency of I Am Creator feels like in form.

- When you exist in the I Am Creator frequency, everything comes to you, everything's clear, everything's easy.

- You are that which you call God, and God is in everything.

CHAPTER FOUR

THE PATH OF THE WAYSHOWER

In this chapter, The Council encourages you to stay conscious and act from your heart because whatever you feel is what you contribute to the world.

We are so pleased and delighted to have the opportunity to speak with you on this glorious day, in this glorious time, as you find yourself in the *absolute knowing* of the mastery that you have over your life experience. You're going to see how this all has led to here and now and *why* you have been on this journey of becoming all that you are. You have been asking to live your purpose. You have been asking to be a wayshower. You have been asking to be of service. We have said to you that this is about living your life fully, allowing your life to be everything that you intended it to be, and *fully loving*—fully loving yourself and fully loving your life experience.

We will begin by reminding you of the transformation experience. You have been going through a decade and then some of transformation, of really moving through the process of changing form, changing perspective, changing physical environment, and changing your reality. As we have said, you are reality. You are reality. *You are reality*, and you're moving through this experience with a perspective of what you draw into your field and into your reality.

We want you to start practicing. This is something new and expanded that we want you to start realizing for yourself. Your brain is never going to understand that everything you experience, your perception of everything, is an *extension of your energy. It's all you.* If you really stay present in the moment, in your consciousness, you can recognize that everything that you perceive is your own energy. There is nothing and no one out there controlling your experience. Nothing is taking energy from you. In fact, no one can take your energy from you, and you need not take energy from others because your energy is all that you ever need in this life experience.

Energy is different from consciousness. This is important. But first, we want you to understand that while there is a difference between energy and consciousness, there is also a place where energy and consciousness are one. Other people are merely a reflection of you and your reality. Understand that while you can perceive a consciousness that is different than yours, everything is *your* energy. Start moving through the world by not creating separation, not going into judgment, but instead by understanding that another person is merely a different consciousness than the consciousness you know as you.

———

While you can perceive a consciousness that is different than yours, everything is your energy.

———

Everything is energy, and consciousness is everything. Your brain works with form, and it's a wonderful thing, because it runs all the systems in your body that keep you alive. It perceives through physical senses what you see, what you hear, what you taste, what you touch, what you smell, and finally, what you think. Thinking is a perceiving mechanism. *Consciousness is not a perceiving mechanism or a sense*, and that is why your brain can't really perceive that another being is consciousness in form.

This relates greatly to what we have been teaching about moving beyond judgment. You can be discerning. You can choose, without judgment, to not entangle. You can recognize that another is of a different consciousness than you without judging them as being wrong or even as being right. You can say, *this feels aligned*. You can say, *this feels good*. But it's not so much the good that trips you up. It's when you perceive that something has gone wrong or that what is happening is bad or out of your control.

The second you see something as bad or terrible or devastating or out of your control, you may go instantly into a state of unconsciousness, of powerlessness, of fear, of overwhelm. In that state you constrict, you resist, you react, you shut down, you have less energy flowing through you. You have a narrower perspective from your state of consciousness. Everything feels awful, terrible, out of control, and you can find yourself in a state of suffering and struggle very quickly.

That is what you have traditionally done. But that is *not* how you have to move forward. It is not really in your reality that the chaos occurs.

There is often a great amount of focus on suffering. There's a great amount of focus on danger. There is a great amount of focus on feeling out of control and unable to manage a threat. Yet we would say to most of you that those things are usually not actually in your reality. You're perceiving others' realities—it's not in your current form or experience.

Now, you might say, *It's happening to people I care about. I'm watching it on the news*. And we understand. However, we want you, all of you, to know you are not helpless; you are not victims. It is more important than ever before that you *stay in the moment*, stay in your power, and stay *conscious*.

———

What creates chaos is a lack of consciousness, a lack of presence, a lack of allowing energy to support you and guide you and flow to you.

———

We understand when something seems to be of a significant magnitude in your life that your thinking begins to affect your emotions, which affects your vibration, which in turn affects your reality. The more *real* it appears to you, the more your thinking begins to affect your emotions. Those emotions begin to affect the way you feel. The way you feel begins to affect your vibration because of the level of energy you allow or disallow based on your emotion. Then you can feel unbalanced, frantic, chaotic, and create suffering within yourself.

We want to give you the highest perspective here. As way-showers, as the highly conscious beings that you are, you have gone through your own transformations in order to create a better way, to guide others. The path you're taking is the path of the wayshower. The way you live your life is how you create a new paradigm.

We who are non-physical, those of us in a higher rate of vibration or a higher state of consciousness, are here to assist you because you are the ones open and allowing your consciousness to be elevated to a higher perspective. You are the ones who are the bridge between much higher states of awareness and conscious-ness and perspective, who bring greater potential and possibilities, and who can pave a better way forward for humankind.

The issues that exist within the human experience are not going to be solved from the perspective of the consciousness that is seeing the issues and the problems or even creating those issues and problems. We want you to understand this. It is important. If you relate all things to consciousness, you will find it very easy to get yourself into a higher perspective or viewpoint of what is occurring in all situations. *There is no problem that has ever been solved from the same perspective or viewpoint that created the problem or the issue.*

——

**There is no problem that has ever been solved
from the same perspective or viewpoint
that created the problem or the issue.**

——

The collective human consciousness is existing within a three-dimensional state of consciousness—not necessarily a different state than you are in, although in time you may begin to find yourself in a different form when you're in a different state of consciousness. However, the issues, challenges, and problems you perceive; the conditions or realities that have resulted from separation, fear, war, judgment, chaos, prejudice; this feeling of *me, me, me* and *I, I, I*; this mentality of *it's all about me and what I want* to satisfy the wound within you—all are *reflected back* in events that occur on your planet. It is essential to recognize this.

What you have done in the past 10 years' time is to go through your own transformation to heal the wounds within you. It may be difficult for you to understand what we are about to say, but the truth is that it doesn't really matter where the wounds came from. This transformation that you have undergone has brought your pain and suffering to the light, has elevated your awareness, your consciousness, to a place where you understand that you're not broken, you're not stuck, you're not what happened in your life. *You are something so much more.* Through all sorts of divinely orchestrated experiences, you have healed great parts of yourself to return to a state of purity. You have gone through your own cleansing to a purification of your thoughts, a purification of your beliefs, a purification of your energy, so that you allow yourself to be in a vibration of joy, peace, and harmony *within you.*

If you want to create anything in the world around you, you must first create it within yourself. If you want to heal the world, you must first heal yourself. If you want to create a more loving, harmonious, beautiful, abundant world around you, *you must first create it within you.* If you will remember this in all times, in all things, and in all circumstances, then the first step is always *you,* not what's going on out there, but what's going on within *you.*

If you begin to focus out there, you lose your own consciousness. You move yourself out of a Fifth Dimension, higher-perspective state of consciousness back into the lower state of consciousness where the problem was created, and then you find yourself in the chaos and in the suffering and in the struggle.

You may ask, *What does the world need of me?* Here is the answer: it needs you to stay conscious. You may ask, *What do those who are suffering need most from me*? It is for you to not get triggered into a state of reaction and resistance. When you begin to suffer in this way, you will contribute to the existing suffering or even create more suffering. What the world needs from you is for you to stay conscious and present in the moment and create within *you* what you most desire in the world around you.

That is why your own transformation has occurred. That is why you have gone through the healing journey you have gone through. That is why everything has led you to this very moment. It's for this time now so that you *really can* be the wayshowers and light up the world when it needs you most.

We have said you are not here to *fix* a broken world. You are not here to *save* the world. You are here bringing consciousness, bringing forth a better way, a higher perspective, using your life as the template for a new paradigm.

The world needs you to stay conscious. Your family needs you to stay conscious. Your friends need you to stay conscious. Your spouse, your lovers, your loved ones—they need you to stay conscious. Your country, your continent, your planet need you to *stay conscious* and act from your heart, allowing your pure energy and a grander perspective to flow through you.

Go within yourself and find what you most want for the world around you. If you want to live in a peaceful, loving, harmonious world, you must first create it within you.

———

If you want to live in a peaceful, loving, harmonious world, you must first create it within you.

———

It is easy for you to get distracted when there is an event of global magnitude where many are suffering and affected. The numbers create an even greater reaction for you. They can bring you to a state of inner chaos and distract you from your path toward higher consciousness and your mission as a wayshower.

Now, we understand. *We understand.* We understand how much you care. We understand how much you love your planet. We understand how much you love the animals, the land, the trees, the plants, the flowers, and the people. We know how much you love the people, your people. We know how much you care, but know that you can stay conscious as you do so. You can stay in your heart, and you must do so. You must stay conscious. You must be what the world needs most from you—consciousness, love, peace, harmony—and you can only find it within you. You can only create it within you. Then it begins to move into your reality, which means it begins to extend from you, the body that is you, into the field and the reality around you.

There's *no limit* to how expansive that can become because there is no limit to how expansive *you* can become. But that expansion occurs only through consciousness and opening and allowing your energy to flow and serve through you.

Think of your own transformation. Many of you had what appeared at the time to be *devastating* transformations—divorce, death, heartbreak, financial ruin, feeling like everything was gone, destroyed. For many of you, at some point in time it felt like everything in your lives had perished, fallen apart, fallen away, that you were alone and that nothing would ever change or get better. At those times you couldn't imagine that it was happening *for* you. You couldn't believe that a loving God would do that to you or understand why you would ever choose to come into a life and experience that. You felt powerless. You felt like a victim. You felt out of control.

Most of you have been there, and *everything in your life* was affected. Then you changed, and when you changed, everything around you changed. As you transformed, everything around you transformed. In time, you began to see that things were happening *for* you, not *to* you, and you began to remember that it was all really for your highest good all along. You just couldn't understand when it felt like it was the worst it could be. You didn't know how it could improve. You certainly couldn't have believed in those times that it was happening for you. In those moments it certainly didn't feel like a gift. Going through a painful loss in the deepest moments of your struggle and suffering and grief, it did not feel like there would ever be anything good that came of it.

———

**Know that everything happens for you, not to you—
and it is all for your highest good.**

———

But there was, wasn't there? There was. You just didn't see the whole picture back then. You couldn't see the higher perspective, the bigger picture. You didn't have a grander viewpoint that *all of that was happening for you*. And you certainly couldn't have imagined that you would be who you are now, know what you know now, and live the life you live now. You couldn't have imagined what was possible for you. But you know *now*. You can perceive this now because of the state of consciousness you're in.

We assure you that your planet is going through its own transformation, and many places are going to go through their own transformations. It may feel scary, but it is not. It is not terrible. It is not the worst thing ever. When it came to your own transformations, you didn't just survive—you learned how to fly. If you allow yourselves now, *you will thrive*. Most of you are thriving and living and loving fully in your power, in a new state of consciousness, in a new state of awareness, which opens a whole new world to you. Heaven on Earth is here and now, we assure you.

If you think of your own transformation, *it is who you became, not what happened to you*. The stories don't really matter. The facts, the dates, they don't really matter. What matters is who you became in your transformation. That's what matters. Are you more loving? Are you healed? Are you whole and worthy? Are you living at a whole new level of fullness and aliveness? That's who you've *become*: a much more open, loving, allowing person. That's who you've become—wiser, more conscious, more aware.

It's about who you *became* in the transformation. You're more *beautiful* than ever before. You're more *abundant* than ever before. You're more *loving* than ever before. You're more *conscious* than ever before. You are.

––––

It's about who you became in your transformation.
You're more beautiful, more abundant, more loving,
and more conscious than ever before.

––––

Once you have undergone the Great Awakening, the great transformation in your own life, everything is different. You don't need to go through that level of transformation again. You don't need to go through that level of awakening again. From a conscious, aligned perspective, you begin to navigate through the human experience and explore different states of consciousness—but from the perspective of a Creator who moves through the world with ease and grace and harmony and joy. Your reality is very different. *The same is true for any and all things that experience transformation.*

In time, places that experience what appear to be traumatic events or natural disasters will appear as lush, flourishing Gardens of Eden. They will be transformed and more beautiful than ever before. Green, abundant, harmonious, beautiful. The people will be forever changed. They will be a society of highly conscious, loving beings. There are problems that will be solved. There are advancements that will occur. There are creations that will result from those experiences that will move your planet forward, that will assist in quantum leaps forward. We assure you.

It will take some time in your human experience, just like your own transformation. What is it that takes the greatest time and healing? What is it that takes the greatest time in transformation or in healing anything? It is simply judgment. If you're judging something that is happening as awful, terrible, bad, devastating, wrong, apocalyptic, and you start going into fear, then you're contributing to the suffering and perpetuating the fear.

Stay in the moment, stay conscious in the situation, and allow your energy to flow. Go within and ask yourself, *What do I most want for the people? What do I most want for the animals? What do I most want for the land?* Remember, you get more of what you *are*. Not what you think you need. Not what you want, not so much. You get *more* of what you *are*, and all that you can give is what you are.

Think about it. Can you give what you need? If you need a glass of water, can you give a glass of water when that's the thing you don't have? If you really are thirsty and you want a glass of water because you do not have a glass of water, then you do not have a glass of water to give.

What you need or what you want must be separate from you, which means you don't have it, which means you cannot give it, which means *you cannot contribute what you do not have.* Really, this is so important. You cannot give what you want, and you cannot give what you need, because in the very wanting and the needing of it you are implying that you don't have it. It's somewhere out there. It's certainly not within you.

You can only give more of what you are. You can only contribute what you are. You can only give what you are. So, you must go within and find what it is that you want to flow through you. Only by looking within can you find what you want to contribute.

Consciousness would be quite helpful in this situation. Love would be quite helpful in this situation. Kindness would be quite helpful. Peace would be quite helpful, maybe more than anything. Peace, love, consciousness.

We know that the word *peace* sometimes feels a bit better than the words *consciousness* or *awareness*. It somehow seems that peace would be a better thing or love would be a better thing. We understand. And from a state of consciousness, you too understand. You get harmony. You get peace. You get love. You get abundance. You get knowing. You get inspiration. You get *all of it* through your state of consciousness.

From your state of consciousness, being completely in the present moment, what is the highest perspective of the situation? See the land as flourishing and green and abundant. See the people as loving and harmonious. See the animals as free and blissful and playful. *Hold that vision*, because when you do it from a conscious perspective in the moment, you are bringing that vision into human consciousness. When more of you do that, you will bring about the great transformation, the Great Awakening, faster than ever before. Not from a place of lack or need or wanting, but because you will know it is here now.

As you create it within your own reality, you make it possible for others to remember that they too can create their own realities. As you move into knowing yourself as the Creator of your life experience, knowing yourself as a sovereign being free to choose the world or reality you create to live in, you seed human consciousness with the potential for all beings to remember that they too are the Creators of their life experiences, that they too can create their own realities, that they too can choose to live in Heaven on Earth.

The simplest way we could give it to you is Heaven on Earth. Energetically, vibrationally, you all can feel into that place, but you must create it within you.

The world you see around you is a reflection of the world that exists within you. The reality that you see around you is a reflection of the reality that exists within you. We'll say it again. The reality you see around you is a reflection of the reality that exists within you. Ask yourself, *Is the world within you Heaven on Earth?* Are your thoughts, your feelings, and your beliefs Heaven on Earth? Are they loving? Are they harmonious? Are they peaceful? Or are they chaotic and devastating and suffering?

**The reality around you is a reflection
of the reality within you.**

———

Only you can create Heaven on Earth within you. As more of you do, you will see reality transformed at a rate you have never before experienced in your human form. Reality transforms because of your consciousness, because of your energy, because of your perspective and awareness.

It's really a waste of time to become lost in devastation and the trauma and the drama and the suffering. *There is a vibrational price you pay when you allow your world to become chaotic and devastating and full of fear and struggle.* You pay a vibrational price. You do. Your body pays the price, and your relationships likely pay the price. Your love pays a price. Your happiness pays a price. There is a vibrational price you pay.

Remember this. *We are not saying that there's anything to fear in the times to come. Quite the opposite.* This is why you're here. This is the greatest time that has *ever* existed in human consciousness. It is because of you that a new reality is forming.

It is because of you that potentials and possibilities are being seeded into human consciousness. It's because of you.

Do you want to live your purpose? Do you want to serve? This is how you do it. If something is in your physical reality that needs your compassion, that needs your assistance, that needs your generosity, do not try to give what you do not have. Align with it within you first, and you will have more. You must elevate yourself beyond the experience of lack or limitation—and you have the ability to do so. Much of giving, helping, assisting, or trying to fix is still done from the three-dimensional state of consciousness, not-enoughness, or a perception of *If I give to you, I no longer have.* Or it is done from an attempt—and it is truly only an attempt—to give what you do not have.

Find it within you first. Get yourself into a conscious state *first*, and then move forward in a state of consciousness from that state of awareness.

If there's chaos in your actual physical state, you must come into a state of consciousness first. Otherwise you're in a reactive mode—reacting, not responding—and you're reacting from a state of resistance, trying to get the chaos to stop, trying to get the powerlessness to stop, trying to solve it even though you feel like a victim. You must come into your power first. You must move into a state of consciousness. That's what it means to be a master of your own life, and those who master their lives will do great things in this world.

We have often spoken to you about the greats, those who have left a legacy, those who have created great change. If you think of those beings, you would consider all of them to be masters, *masters of the human experience*. Jesus, Buddha, Gandhi, Martin Luther King, Jr., Saint Francis, Mother Teresa. Many, many. So many. There really have been so many, most of whom you *don't* know by name, and they navigated through this human experience with their own level of consciousness. Now, you can navigate through this human experience with *your* own level of consciousness.

The energy that creates worlds is you. It's you. There's nothing out there taking your energy. There's nothing out there that *can* take your energy. You can, however, limit or constrict your energy through the thoughts you have. It's almost always your judgment that creates a *thinking* that what's going on is terrible, bad, devastating, horrible, horrific, and wrong, wrong, wrong.

That's what shifts you into a state of consciousness that's no longer necessary for you. We're just going to say it that way. *It's no longer necessary.* Yes, everything serves. You can't get it wrong. It's not that big of a deal, as you've heard us say, if you go into a state of unconsciousness. With practice, it's easier to get yourself back into a state of consciousness and awareness.

That is the first and most important step. From there you ask, *What is needed?* Then you ask, *What do I want?* When you look at any situation, what do you want? What do you want for the people, the land, or the animals that you see in that situation? What do you want for them? Maybe it is peace. Maybe it is love. Maybe it is comfort.

Feel it within you. Feel it in every cell of your body. Really take the moment, take the time, whether it takes a minute or an hour or a day. That's the first and most important part in creating change, especially great change. Feel comfort within *you*. Feel peace within *you*. Feel love within *you*. Go to the highest perspective. See the land, the people, and the animals living in a state of Heaven on Earth. Lush, harmonious, and abundant. The highest of well-being for all. Then once you're aligned, once you feel that, you can extend it from you and expand it from you.

Here are a couple of things you can do since you probably want to *do* something. First, go within and allow yourself to *feel,* and feel deeply. As we said, the world you see around you is a reflection of the world that exists within you. The reality around you is created by the reality within you. As you hold the vision, you can focus from your heart to the hearts of others. You can infuse the feeling of peace into the light that you extend out into the world, and we promise you, it is *absolutely* seeding human consciousness—and everything and all things in the human experience—with a grander possibility of living in Heaven on Earth. In those moments they might not know why they feel a sense of peace or comfort, but it makes it possible for those who are in some unwanted experience to find peace and comfort.

The other thing that you can *do* is take your state of presence, consciousness, awareness—your state of being aligned with peace, with comfort and peace and harmony and love—and extend that to everything that is in your reality. *Actually* in your reality. Not on the TV, not on the Internet, not in the newspaper. What is actually in your reality. This is really important.

Align your consciousness with a state of comfort, peace, harmony, and love. Then extend that to everything that is actually in your reality.

There are people in your reality. There are animals in your reality. There are trees in your reality. There is land in your reality *right here, right now* that would be served positively by you contributing a greater sense of peace within your reality. And *that* will have a ripple effect. That will begin to spread healing and love and peace and joy and comfort and well-being all throughout the human experience. *But you must start with where you are and what is in your reality now.* If you're looking to the news or to what is far away, you will feel helpless.

There is so much you can do to assist here and now. Do not overlook that. You do not serve anyone or anything by going into a state of powerlessness or helplessness or utter fear and chaos and grief—*except* for in those moments when that level of discomfort causes you to *focus on a desired outcome and start aligning with it.* That distinction is important.

We hold no judgment if you ever go into states of fear or suffering or chaos. We absolutely are always, always, always in the highest perspective, holding the vision for the highest good of all. And so it is. From our perspective, it is done. How long it takes you to align with what you want and create it within your reality is up to you. From our perspective, it is done. It is our reality, and it can be yours, and it can be *anyone's* who chooses it.

Just because many parts of the world will begin to move into a more loving, harmonious way of being and existing and thriving and flourishing on this planet does not mean that all beings do not have the free will to choose the world they live in. They do have free will, but remember that what you experience now doesn't have to be your world. You're responsible for the reality that you create within you, and that is the reality you will experience around you.

We say this all with such great love for you. We say this all absolutely knowing the power you have to create great change in the world around you. Not because something is wrong, but because you are seeding human consciousness with greater potential and possibilities, because you are the wayshower and the way you live your life is the path. The path is what you are giving. Who you have become is what you give to the world around you. The healed, whole, healthy, thriving, loving, caring, beautiful, satiated being that you are—*that's* your gift to the world.

Anything and everything is possible for you. Anything and everything is possible for *everyone*. Those of you who now understand the significance of your own transformations, and that they are leading you to assist humanity through its great transformation, should feel really good. When you really get how important you are, the power you have, the love that you are, how free you are, how perfect it is, and how perfect you are, you'll say: *Thank you, thank you, thank you. Thank you for my life. Thank you for this life. Thank you for all life. Thank you for the opportunity to be here now. Thank you for helping me remember the I Am That I Am, the master that I am over my life experience. Thank you, thank you.* And you will move forward, and you will love like you have never loved before. You will love like you have never loved before, and you will shine like you have never shined before. And you will *live* like you have never lived before. You will.

———

**When you really understand how important you are,
you will live like you have never lived before.**

———

We love you so very much. We say this all with such great love for who you are, for your journey, and for who you have become.

ESSENTIAL MESSAGES

- If you stay present in the moment, in your consciousness, you can recognize that there are other consciousnesses, but that everything that you perceive is your own energy. Nothing out there is controlling your experience. Nothing is taking energy from you.

- The path you're taking is the path of the wayshower. The way you live your life is how you create a new paradigm.

- If you want to create anything in the world around you, you must first create it within yourself. The first step is always you—not what's going on out there, but what's going on within you.

- You can only contribute what you are. You can only give what you are. Remember, you get more of what you already are.

- How long it takes you to align with what you want and create it within your reality is up to you. From our perspective, it is done. It is our reality, and it can be yours. And it can be anyone's who chooses it.

- This is the greatest time that has *ever* existed in human consciousness. It is because of you that a new reality is forming.

- The energy that creates worlds is you. It's you. There's nothing out there that *can* take your energy.

CHAPTER FIVE

THE MOST EXTRAORDINARY LIFE IMAGINABLE

In this chapter, The Council emphasizes how easy it is to master the human experience from a higher state of consciousness, where so much more is possible than you ever imagined.

We are so pleased and delighted to have the opportunity to be here with you on this *extraordinary* day. Extraordinary, extra ordinary, extra special, extra exciting, extra magnificent. That's where your lives are going. Your opportunities for the extraordinary experience of life and living an extraordinary life, a miraculous life, a magical life, lie in this moment—here and now.

There's nothing for you to achieve before you live an extraordinary life. There is no level of achievement. There's no badge of honor you must receive. You need no one's permission to live an extraordinary life at the highest level, living your fullest potential in your life *every day*, which means experiencing the fullness of all that you are in every moment.

Stop trying to figure it out. Stop trying to achieve. Stop trying to get to that moment where you are anointed or crowned with the medal of enlightenment. Stop trying to figure it out, and live and be and allow it, allow it, allow it. You're already enlightened. You're already realized. You were before you came here. You were, and you have been in this incredible experience of form and exploring different levels of density. It's amazing, isn't it?

Do you really love your life? Do you really love life and the human experience? As we have said, all great mastery involves great love. There isn't anyone who ever mastered anything without love. To master a talent, to master an ability, to master even a relationship takes *great love*. Great love. You want to master your life experience, but do you really, really love the human experience? Do you really love life? Do you really love living?

———

If you want to master your life, you must really love the human experience.

———

Some of you can say yes to that. Some of you are still unsure, which means that you're not allowing yourself to recognize and receive *all* the beauty, *all* the creation, *all* the brilliance, *all* the magnificence that is *here for you*.

We know your human mind still can't quite grasp that this is all here for you. It's all here for you—for you to love, for you to enjoy, for you to find beauty in, and to delight in. It's all here for you so that you can have fun, so that you can create, so that you can play. It's all here so that you can relate to reality. You can even pretend that it's not you, pretend that it's somehow separate from you, and in that way you can find curiosity and new experiences and new levels of awareness of *all that you are*.

Your reality is an extension of you. Do you love *you*? Do you love your reality? Do you love the extension of you that's all around you? Love it. Love it. *Love it.* When you really love it, you allow yourself to emerge into a level of awareness of your magnificence and your innocence like never before. You emerge into an awareness of your power, knowing that you never need to force anything again. You emerge into a new level of awareness of your power without needing to force or control or manipulate or figure anything out.

How great would that be? How great would it be if every day were magical? How great would it be if everything that you related to every day reflected a brilliance to you, as a miraculous, magical reflection of your playfulness, of your innocence, of your absolute joy, *your absolute joy?*

Some of you would say, *Well, I can't really love life because of these circumstances, these conditions, these people I'm relating to, these things I'm relating to, this job I'm relating to, or this world that I can't relate to because it's so different from me and not the way I want it to be.* Yet your focus on that just keeps you in an experience where what you relate to feels so different from you.

It's not. It's just your opportunity for clarity, for confidence, for certainty. Isn't that what you want? Isn't that how you want to live your life? With *clarity*, with *confidence*, with *certainty?* With total trust in yourself, your power, your ability to stay conscious, your ability to stay present in the moment, and in your ability to stay open and allow and receive in every moment?

There's not one of you—not any one of you—who has yet received even a *small* amount of all the goodness that is here for you. Part of being a great master of your life is to fully receive all that is here for you, knowing everything is an extension of you—there's no separation. But again, when you go into judgment, fear, or worry, you separate yourself from everything that's here for you. You create a gap. You know that what is here for you is out there. But you're *here*, and it's not here with you, not where you want it, and you're not where you want to be. So you start trying to figure it out, and you start trying to push and force and manipulate and control and make it all happen your way.

Hear this loud and clear: When you're in lower dimensions of consciousness, when you are in resistance and reaction, you are going to move yourself down into a state of consciousness where lack and separation and fear exist. If you allow yourself to stay open and present and conscious, you will easily be in the vibration where there are higher dimensional emotions, where you open fully to all your power, to all that is here for you, and you allow yourself to receive, receive, *receive.*

What are you receiving? We say that you receive, but what are you receiving? Well, you're receiving the only thing that's in everything. *Energy.* Fear is not in everything. Energy is in everything. Money is energy. Healing is energy. Your body is energy. Your relationships are energy. They are. Everything is energy. You are energy. And everything is consciousness. You expand your consciousness by allowing more energy.

Consciousness is where it's all at. Consciousness and energy are where it's all at because this life experience is easy to master when you are in a higher state of consciousness. From higher states of consciousness this life experience is *quite simple*. It can be everything you intend it to be. You can be everything that you are. You will love your life in a way you never ever thought possible because before, you were so focused on all the things that you had to have and had to do and had to change. You were so focused on all the circumstances that you needed to figure out in order to get your life to a certain level so that you could love it, instead of just allowing it *right now.*

———

From a higher state of consciousness, this life experience is easy to master, and it can be everything you intended it to be.

———

That's what the master of one's own life knows. The master knows consciousness, and the master knows energy. Now the master knows how to merge them into the greatest level of power and the greatest level of openness and allowing so that they can receive anything and everything that is here in this moment, to serve them and to serve through them.

All of you desire deeply to be in service. It is not an expectation, but you are at levels of consciousness where you deeply desire to contribute, to serve, to make a difference, to make it better, to make it easier. Most of you even hold the vision of contributing to the Great Awakening of humanity, to the elevation into New Earth, to the Great Ascension. You all want to serve in positively contributing to raising the vibration of the planet, to raising the consciousness level of the planet.

You know what's coming, don't you? To do that you have to raise *your own consciousness*. That's the only way. If you want to raise the energy to access New Earth or to access the Great Awakening, you have to raise your own energy. To positively contribute to raising the consciousness level on the planet, you have to raise your own. That is the greatest way you serve. That is the greatest way you contribute.

Yes, yes, yes, there will be things that you do, groups that you serve, people that you lead, and there will be projects and services and products that you share with the world. But do not forget the most important piece of it all is *your* consciousness and where *your* energy is; you're open and allowing your energy to flow through you and to serve you and to serve through you so you can elevate your consciousness to the highest level. That's it. You *will* serve in raising the consciousness level of humanity.

You can do all of this without ever again entangling with trauma, drama, suffering, or lower-dimensional emotions where you move back into density and struggle. You can transcend it at any moment. *Don't try to figure it out. Don't try to force it.* It only happens through opening and allowing. Open and allow your joy. Open and allow your beauty. Open and allow inspiration and creativity. Open your heart. Open your eyes. Open your arms up wide. Say *yes* to this day, say *yes* to your life, say *yes* to loving your life and loving this world and loving this human experience. That's all it takes!

No badge of honor. No specific achievement. No passing any test. No waiting for someone to anoint you and give you permission. If you need it, you have permission, but it's the permission you give yourself. It's permission to the Self, the capital *S* Self. You are giving permission to the Self, the part of you that *is* consciousness, the part of you that *is* energy, the part of you that has never forgotten who you really are and knew how perfect you were and how perfect this experience was—even when the human you had forgotten. It's coming home to you, giving permission to the Self, opening and allowing all that you are and all your power and all that is here for you.

We understand it's a practice. It is simple, almost so simple your human brain wants it to be more difficult. And because it's not more difficult, you just go back and do the difficult stuff. It takes a lot of work to hold yourself in density. It takes *a lot of work* to be in suffering and pain and struggle. It really does. That's what creates work. It takes a lot of work.

————

It takes a lot of work to hold yourself in density.

————

It doesn't have to be that hard, but you're given this magnificent ability to think and perceive and to conceptualize and to analyze and to memorize. *You have free will to think anything you choose.* Consider that when you think terrible, awful thoughts about yourself or others or about your world or when you think hopeless thoughts or mean thoughts. That's how free you are.

If you think of animals, for example, most of you would say that in the presence of an animal you feel their pure Source Energy. You feel their innocence, you feel their love, you feel this sentient being that's so divine. You marvel in the animals so much because they are closer to pure Source Energy, because most of the time they're completely and totally open and allowing, because *they're not limiting energy through their thinking by dragging themselves into lower dimensions of consciousness.*

Now, we would agree that some animals that go through certain experiences or traumatic experiences also take on limitation. We're not going to say that you transmute heavy, dense, negative emotions and thinking onto animals. However, they are very domesticated for most of you, living in your space and continuously exposed to your consciousness, and they begin to be more susceptible to what's going on in your field of consciousness.

The greatest thing that you could do for your animals is to open and allow your own energy, to expand your *own* consciousness, to be in a state of peace and joy and love and freedom and openness, and less in your thinking mind. If you did, you would notice that communication with the animals would become easier. Even if you thought you didn't have the ability to communicate with animals, you would start noticing that you do.

This is *oneness*. This is an expansion of your consciousness, of what's possible. This is also beginning to elevate your experience beyond a lot of the limitation that you perceive. Communicating in verbal, spoken words is actually a limitation that you experience in density because of how your human mind processes information. The animals are always communicating with you, just like all of those in the non-physical plane are always with you and always available to you and always communicating with you. But animals are at such a rate of vibration that your *physical senses* don't really pick up the lightness or the subtleness or the high frequency of their communication or their presence. The next level down from that would be nature, and the next level down from that would be animals. Then the next level down from that is human communication.

Let's talk about nature. As you start tuning into being able to communicate through your consciousness and your vibration with animals, you begin to open yourself up to nature and the natural world around you and the wisdom in it, the knowledge that exists there, the intelligence that exists there, and the communication that's always available to you. You can start co-creating, collaborating, and connecting to nature and all that is here for you on such a deeper level.

The trees are part of systems. The trees are part of intelligence. They're part of ancient wisdom. The land, the fields, the grass, the mountains, the oceans—they all carry wisdom. They all carry knowledge, and they all carry consciousness. *You can start harmonizing with all of that.* There is also a whole unseen-by-the-human-eye world of intelligence that exists all around you all the time. That's what you call divine orchestration or even magic—magical things. That's why you tend to associate things like unicorns and fairies and elementals as this sort of magical Source and the magical world, the fantasy world, the fairy-tale world.

Don't you all want the fairy-tale world? That doesn't mean you're not grounded and conscious and present in the moment. It means *precisely* that. When you're grounded and present and conscious in the moment and open and allowing, you expand your life. All sorts of worlds start opening and presenting themselves to you and becoming a resource to you, an opportunity for you to expand more than you ever thought was possible from a human perspective. You think you love life *now*? Just wait. Oh, just wait until you *really* start allowing magical and miraculous things to present themselves to you.

When you're grounded, present, and conscious, all sorts of worlds start presenting themselves to you as an opportunity to expand what you thought was possible from a human perspective.

This is it. This is why you're here. This is what you've been preparing for. This is why you have come to the place of remembering. *You are creating the New Earth. You are creating Heaven on Earth.* Although, we will say—and your human mind might not quite understand what we mean by this—you already created it. You just stepped into physical form to experience it because *it's the best thing ever.*

Of course, in a New Earth or Heaven on Earth there's *more*. There's more than what is in the lower dimensions of consciousness within the human experience. There's more. And it's not about an illusion. It's not about a level of magic and mastery where you perform tricks or use your supernatural talents to entertain others or to fix others or to change others or to do what you think needs to be done. No, it's not any of that. It's opening and allowing and living at a level of mastery where you have *absolutely redefined* what's possible. Through you living your fullest potential and expanding what is possible, you seed human consciousness and the human experience with these greater potentials and possibilities. All from a place of being fully grounded, fully present, fully conscious, in the now moment, in the human experience, and expanding it with your consciousness, your awareness, and your energy.

It's not about doing the impossible because doing the impossible takes a lot of force. It's not about any of that. It's about *reimagining* what's possible, *redefining* what's possible, *reprogramming* yourself about what you know, rather than what you believe is possible.

Are you starting to get excited about your life? Are you starting to get *really* excited about where this is all going? Indeed. All that's left to do is open up and allow and love yourself and love your life and be here now, conscious and present in every moment. *Allow* your awareness to open up to more. That is how you *serve* in the Great Awakening. That is how you positively contribute to expanding human consciousness. That is how you elevate the vibration on the planet. Through you.

We'll just take one more opportunity to help you really shift and understand this conversation around consciousness. Everything on the planet that you deem as wrong and bad is merely a matter of consciousness. Some of you still think consciousness is about what sort of food you choose or don't choose to eat. Some of you think consciousness is still about a particular political party that's more conscious than the other—about *what*? Some of you believe that consciousness is still very much about how to manifest more stuff.

———

Everything that you deem as wrong and bad is merely a matter of consciousness.

———

It's all of that, yes. However, *that's not really what we're talking about.* There are multiple different levels of consciousness. We're just guiding you to open up to the highest level of consciousness possible in the human experience, the grandest perspective, so that you have the highest viewpoint, and in *that* you will serve in the greatest possible ways and contribute in ways that your human brain will never understand.

We don't want you to think about struggle, suffering, challenges, or problems in the same way that you have been doing so until now. We want you to think about them from a viewpoint of consciousness. It's just where the consciousness is in that place at that time. It's just where that person's consciousness is in that place at that time. There's nothing wrong; it's not bad, and it doesn't need to be fixed.

We understand from our viewpoint where your consciousness has been at different points of time, and there's no judgment from our side ever. You even know when you have been in different states of consciousness at different times. You know the level of suffering that occurred when you were in lower states of consciousness, the choices you made, the trauma and the drama and the suffering that was created from the lack of consciousness. It wasn't you being bad or doing something wrong that you were somehow going to get punished for or create negative karma about. No. It was just your state of consciousness at that time.

Part of the free-will experience is your ability to determine how much energy you're opening and allowing at any time, which determines the level of consciousness you're in. You have the free will to choose the thoughts you're thinking, you have the free will to create the beliefs you want to create, and you have the free will to create your reality. You have it all.

We know everything in your world—political parties, government, starvation, poverty, incarceration, victims, powerlessness—*seems* like a big deal, but they are all just a different state of consciousness. They are not the truth of who you are. You're energy—and you're consciousness.

There really isn't anything more important than you staying open and allowing energy to serve you and to serve through you. But we don't want to talk to you about letting energy serve through you quite yet, because you will start to get into expectations and specifics. You look around, judging what's not right and what needs to be fixed and who needs to be healed, and then you start flowing energy to them. That's not what we're talking about. We want you to really *master* allowing energy from a state of innocence and being fully impeccable, which is just to open and allow and receive and stay conscious and present. Feel it. Be present to the energy.

———

Nothing is more important than staying open and allowing energy to serve you and serve through you. Master allowing energy from a state of innocence and being fully impeccable.

———

Innocence means you're free. Innocence means you're lighthearted. All is well. You're joyful, and you're uplifted. There's that twinkle in your eye, and there's that radiance about you. That's innocence. Anytime you need to open up to your innocence, shift your gaze up to the sky, look up toward the sun or the beautiful clouds in the sky or the moon or the stars and *smile*.

There's this whole big universe, and then there's you. You're the center of the universe, and the *whole* universe is here for you. If that does not shift you into a state of innocence, what will? When you're standing in nature and looking at the mountains and the trees and the birds, and you're standing there seeing magnificence and the beauty and all the perfection in it all and you know it's an extension of you and it's all here for you, *that's* innocence.

Innocence is oneness. Innocence is pure love. Innocence is allowing your pure light to shine through you. Being impeccable means that you do not drag yourself down into lack and limitation and separation and create a gap in order to create and practice mastery, to stay in a state of being impeccable, in alignment or in accordance with the highest good, the highest standard, the highest perspective, the highest viewpoint that you know you can align to from your state of innocence. But you can't understand it from your human thinking mind. Your human thinking mind can't figure out the bigger picture, can't figure out the highest perspective, and is *never going to figure out* what's going on. As you expand your consciousness and awareness, you'll feel into it and you'll know, but it's not because your human mind figured it out. It's not because your human mind achieved a state of enlightenment. That's not it at all.

Open and allow energy. Fully receive. Allow energy to serve *you*. Stay in a state of innocence. Stay in a state of being impeccable. Allow your consciousness to expand. Allow your awareness to expand. Be here, be present, feel all your power like never before, and love yourself, love this moment, love your life, love this world, love this human experience. Oh, and then watch what it's like to live the most magical and miraculous and extraordinary life you could ever possibly imagine. And so it is.

———

Allow your consciousness to expand, and you will live the most extraordinary life imaginable.

———

We love you so much. We love you so much. We know there is intensity in our message to you, but *it is the most intense love and knowing of the truth of who you are.*

ESSENTIAL MESSAGES

- If you want to raise the energy to access New Earth or the Great Awakening, you must raise your own energy. To positively contribute to raising consciousness on the planet, you've got to raise your own.

- Allowing yourself to receive all that is here for you is so simple that your human brain wants it to be more difficult. Because it's not more difficult, you just go back and make it difficult. It takes a lot of work to hold yourself in density.

- When you're grounded, present, and conscious in the moment and open and allowing, you expand your life, and all sorts of worlds start opening themselves up to you.

- It's not about doing the impossible, because doing the impossible takes a lot of force. It's about reimagining what's possible, redefining what's possible.

- Your human thinking mind can't figure out the bigger picture, can't figure out the highest perspective, and is never going to figure out what's going on. But as you expand your consciousness and awareness, you'll feel into it—and you'll know.

CHAPTER SIX

LIVING IN HARMONY WITH YOUR DESTINY

In this chapter, The Council assures you that there is a divine plan and that you are always free to choose. When you are living in alignment to the divine plan, your destiny is choiceless. It is beyond your wildest dreams.

We are so pleased and delighted to have the opportunity to speak with you all on this fine and glorious day indeed. This is a celebration of all that you are, a celebration of this time now, and a celebration for the most incredible opportunity of a lifetime, which is to be here now and to open and receive the love, the wisdom, the joy, the happiness, the fun, the peace, the play, the creation that is here for all of you, here in this now.

We celebrate each and every one of you at all times and in every moment because you are the brave and courageous ones who stepped forth into the human experience to bring to humanity what is needed most—more love and more light. You really are the light of the world. You are the bright, beautiful lights illuminating the world just by being who you are.

Many of you are feeling the expansion of awareness that is happening. Many of you are feeling the expanded amounts of energy that you are beginning to allow into your physical bodies. You are opening up. You are expanding, and you are letting more of all that you are be here and now, which means your soul, your higher self, that grander part of you, the I Am Presence frequency. There is really nothing better than the *I Am That I Am* being fully present in your life at this time.

Indeed, there is a grander plan here. We don't want you to get so wrapped up in it so that you are waiting for destiny to show up for you, but we do want to assure you always that there is so much here for you. There is a grander, more expansive plan for your life, for this journey, for this time here and now in the Earth experience.

There is a grand plan. You *are* supported. You *are* assisted. You are provided for beyond your wildest dreams. You cannot even imagine; you cannot even think to *ask* for what you will experience in your lives in these coming times. You cannot think to dream that big. You cannot think to ask that big. You cannot even pray out loud for what is coming for you, which is destined for you but *has been here all along*. It's the perfect convergence of the most unlimited potential and possibilities for your life coming into the now moment—you, fully realizing yourself as the Creator of your life experience and yet knowing that the you, the human you, could have never even asked for how good it is and how good it's going to get.

———

You are provided for beyond your wildest dreams.
You cannot even imagine what you will experience.

———

When we say there is a divine plan and there is destiny, it is known by your soul, your higher self. It is known by the collective consciousness that is always guiding and supporting you. But we don't want your human self to feel like it doesn't have full opportunities in every moment to choose, to experience, the freedom of being here and now.

That is why we say to you that it is *choiceless*. It doesn't mean you don't have a choice. It doesn't mean that there are no options. It just means in those moments that you will know with such certainty, with such clarity, exactly the next perfect step that is on your path, that is your destiny, because it will just be choiceless. *You will know.* The path will light up. It will just be *so clear.* There will be such certainty.

At times you have heard us say "that or something better"— asking for "that or something better." It is only *something better* because your human self could not even imagine to ask for the better thing, to imagine the potential and the possibilities that are available. Why? Because your human self is still sifting and sorting and shifting through the limitation learned in this life experience.

Every single one of you, hear this now. Think of every dream that you've had until now, every vision that you've had for your life until now, everything that you *thought* was your destiny. Now know that there is a clean slate for you to start from the most limitless potential and possibility for your life, and to move forward *never again* needing to move your desires, your dreams, your destiny into limitation for you to experience the most beautiful, magical, miraculous creation within form.

Many of your dreams and desires and wishes have been based on avoiding unwanted circumstances, or you had some intuition years ago about something and you thought that must be it, that must be it, that *must* be it. But you have a clean slate now to never again experience the delay or the gap between you and your highest potential, your destiny here and now. It's better than you can imagine. It's better than you can ask for. This is our favorite part: *you're never going to figure it out.* You're never going to figure it out. That's the fun of it. Isn't that the joy? Isn't that *really* part of the fun of the human experience, that every single day, every moment holds the potential and the possibility for a miracle, for magic, for the most divinely orchestrated, *beautiful* creations and manifestations to present themselves to you?

The really fun part of the human experience is that every moment holds the possibility for miracles, magic, and divinely orchestrated, beautiful creations.

———

What is your role in all of this? Many of you still ask as if you do not know. *Who am I? Why am I here? What is my purpose?* Many of you are allowing yourselves to expand your awareness of a deeper knowing and understanding of the answers to those questions.

This moment right here, right now, has never existed before and will never exist again. You, in this moment, have never existed before. The you that you know as you right here, right now, has never existed before and will never exist again. Just for a moment from this place, this clean slate, this here and now moment that has never existed before and will never exist again, ask yourself: Who *am* I? Who am I? Who am I?

We'll tell you the answer to that question. You are All That Is and all that will ever be. You are the highest good. You are the grandest potential. You are the greatest possibility. You are the most beautiful, magical, magnificent thing that you will ever create. You are perfection expressing itself in physical form. You are the Source. You are the Divine. You are God. You are all of it. You are here in physical form to experience you and all that you are, and the journey will always, always lead you back to you. Everything that you want, everything that you desire, every experience you want to have, it will all lead you back to you—a more expanded version of you, a greater expression of you, a deeper knowing of you, a deeper loving of you. *It all leads back to you.*

You are All That Is and all that will ever be. You are the Source. You are the Divine. You are all of it.

Many of you connect to guides. Many of you connect to archangels and Ascended Masters, the greats that walked your planet. Many of you connect to loved ones on non-physical planes. Many of you are more open and aware of your connection to the animals and to the land and to the elementals and to the many other higher-dimensional beings that are supporting your journey in this experience of form. If you could really see it from our perspective—to know who you are and why you're here and what your purpose is—you would know yourself as All That Is and all that ever will be here and now, fully living and loving the grandest version of you.

If you sit in the center of your universe, here and now in this moment, as the fullness of all that you are, the perfection of all that you are, and from this moment you expand the light that you are out in every direction, that's what draws more energy to you. It's *all* your energy, and it's *all* your light because you are All That Is. Everything *out there* is just an extension of you. It's just an extension of you. There is other consciousness, there are other experiences, but there's nowhere that you are not because you are the light of the world. You are All That Is. Everything is an extension of you, and everything is here to play with you on this journey back to you. It's all here for you.

Let yourself expand to the corners and the edges of the universe for just a moment. Expand your awareness, expand what you think is possible, expand your vibration, expand your consciousness, expand this moment in the force field that is you. Expand the field so that there's nowhere that you are not—because it's all you. You don't need to understand it. You don't need to be able to explain it. *Just feel it.*

Just feel it. It's all here. It's all you. You are All That Is. Everything is here for your enjoyment, for your appreciation, for your love, for your feelings of love and joy and beauty and fun and playing and creating. All you have to do is to live beyond the limitation that you learned, live beyond the fear and the doubt and the worry, live beyond the belief that you are ever separate from anything because you are not. You are All That Is, and All That Is is here for you, and All That Is is here to serve you, and All That Is serves through you when you fully open and allow the energy that *is you*. That is you. That is you.

———

Everything is here for you to remember who you truly are and to guide you on the journey back to you.

———

The sun is shining for you. The trees are here for you, so big and strong. Majestic mountains are here for you. The air you breathe is here for you. When you look into the eyes of another, they're there for you. It's all here for you to enjoy and to remember who you are so that you can see yourself, so that you can know yourself—Creator within your own creation. All here for you.

You're moving into a time of knowing yourself at a level you've never known yourself before in form, knowing yourself as the most beautiful creation, knowing that you are the most beautiful thing that you will ever create and that all things are an extension of you, here to play with you, on your journey of you. It's the journey of you. While there are some specific things that you have chosen as your destiny, while there is a divine plan, you're *choosing* your experience. At this point, there's no way you could miss out on your destiny because of the level of awareness and consciousness that you are living in. We have said this many different ways to you each time as you were ready to hear it, as you were ready to hear more, and as you were ready to move into greater levels of realization. There is a divine plan, and you're free.

When you understand that from the level of awareness and consciousness you're living in, fully allowing all your energy and allowing energy to serve through you, shining the bright, beautiful light that you are and living your life to the fullest, you will live in such harmony with your destiny. You will live in total harmony with the divine plan. You will live in total alignment to the Source, to the grander plan that's going on here, and you shall do so with such ease and such grace because you live in the flow. There are no choices to make. Each step will be *choiceless* because you realize the only place you ever go is to journey deeper within yourself.

We have said from the very beginning this is a *coming home*, coming home to you. Come home to you, to all that you are and to all that is here for you. Come home, come home to you. It's all here for you now. When you sit and stand and live and breathe from the center of the universe, knowing that *everything is an extension of you*, everything is part of the field where you are expressing and experiencing and exploring and expanding, then if something is out there somewhere, you don't create the gap. You feel into your field. You feel into your force field where it already is because there's no gap.

Imagine there's someone whom you love, and in this moment they are not in your physical proximity, they are not in the same room, they are not in the same house, they are not in the same town, they are not in the same state or country, they're somewhere *out there*—at least that's what you have learned. But if in the moment, instead of perceiving the absence of them when your physical senses tell you that they're not nearby, you look around, call out their name, search everywhere in your physical proximity, the realization that they are not nearby would be more intense, more painful. And when you finally understand that, you perceive separation and feel suffering, and you experience missing them. Because you have free will and because you are choosing your experience, you will create the reality that they are gone and you are separate and you're missing them. But the truth is they're not. They're in your field. They're here! If you start perceiving and sensing your connection to them as *never separate*, you will start experiencing a reality of them, and they you, where there is no separation.

The divine playmate is never separate from you. Your soul family, your angels, your guides, your loved ones, your dear ones, the animals you love, the people you love, the beings you love—they are never separate from you. You've just been perceiving through separation and limitation that they're not here, but they are. As you start perceiving beyond the limitations of the physical senses, you start expanding your potential. You start expanding your possibilities. You allow a whole new reality to emerge through your perception of something *beyond*. All that takes is your awareness. All it takes is awareness because that's expanding your *light*. It's expanding your *consciousness*. That's what expands your *potential*. That's what starts creating a new and even more glorious reality to reveal itself to you. There's no illusion. There's no veil. It's just your awareness, your consciousness, and your light. It's your perception of reality being *all* that it can be.

———

**As you start perceiving beyond the
limitations of the physical senses, you allow
a whole new reality to emerge.**

———

Your human self still can't understand who you really are. It still doesn't know who you really are. We are you. You are us. We've never been separate from you. You're drawing *you* to you. The love is yours. The wisdom is yours. The consciousness is yours. The energy is yours. The light is yours. It has been all along. It's you. It's about you realizing *you* and then you stepping into the life of the master that you came here to be.

Your destiny is that of a master. It *is*, or you wouldn't be reading this. You wouldn't have drawn you here to remind you of the master that you are and to remind you of the potential for your human experience, for the endless, infinite, *eternal* possibilities that are here for you. The only thing that limits them is your entanglement. Entangling with limitation, entangling with lack, entangling with separation, from the God, from the Source, from the light, from the energy that is *you*.

God is everything. God is All That Is. God is eternal. God is the greatest power. God is love. God is All That Is. God is the Divine. It is the Source and Source Energy. It is Source Energy that creates worlds. *That is what you are*, and you're so powerful, *so very* powerful that you can actually create the reality that you are *just* a human, just the limitation that you have believed yourself to be.

Your beliefs create your reality, your perception, how you perceive. You have *no idea* how powerful you are—yet. Power from a perspective that implies force or control over others or circumstances never really did create anything. *Truly*, it didn't. Power from a force perspective never really created or miscreated anything, because it's all light and it's all energy and it's all you.

You're still stepping into understanding power and wisdom. Why would you ever fear your power? You could never really destroy yourself. You never *really* harm yourself. You never really could. Yes, you can do harm to yourself as a human, to the human body. You could do harm to others, but not to *the real part*. Not to the real part *ever*. You can't really hurt or destroy or harm the real part of you or anyone. Your fear of your power is quite silly because you could never really destroy the light. You can never really destroy the Source, the *real* Creator within your own creation.

It's *you*. It's all you. You're expanding your awareness of what it means to be Creator within your own creation and to never, ever, ever fear your power because it is light, it is the Source, and all you have to do is allow it to be so. All you have to do is *let it in*. But it cannot exist in the same place as worry, doubt, and separation. It cannot exist in the same place.

Your capacity is not limited, but part of what you're doing is expanding the channel and the vessel that is you in form to allow more of all that you are, which is All That Is, to flow through you while expressing yourself in the physical plane. If you think of yourself as a container, if you think of yourself as a vessel or a channel, the more you will expand your field, the more you will expand that channel. The more you expand that field, the more light and power you will allow through you.

Could you ever be afraid of the light? No, you're not afraid of light, so don't be afraid of your power because all it is, is light. All it is, is energy. All it is, is energy.

The perception or the misuse or the manipulation of power in the physical experience is nothing but the misunderstanding of what you really are and how power really works. When you get this, oh, it all changes! You begin to really, really, *really* allow the light and the energy that you are to serve you, to serve through you. There's nowhere else to be than in the moment because it's all here, in this force field, in this moment, and you begin to *really* play and *really* delight and *really* dance with all of creation.

There's nothing left to do but play and have fun here, to dance your dance, to have fun, to laugh. Really, there's nothing else. There's no more healing, fixing, processing, doing, forcing, manipulating, figuring it out. None of that. While it all serves, and while it all leads you back to you, you can transcend right here, right now, forevermore any need to move your creations down into density. You can realize the manifestation of *your* Heaven on Earth with everything, *everything* that you deeply desire to experience—Creator within your own creation.

———

There's nothing left to do but play and have fun here, to dance your dance, to have fun, to laugh.

———

Sit with that. Feel that. Live from there, expand from there, express from there. Who are you? You are Heaven on Earth. Why are you here? For Heaven on Earth. What is your purpose? *Heaven on Earth.*

We cannot say this enough. We can't say it in enough ways. *You are* the New Earth. You're here. You're the New Earth. You are. You create the paradigm that exists within *your* Heaven on Earth.

You create the body, the relationships, the ventures, the experiences. Create them in Heaven on Earth with all those divine playmates that are also in Heaven on Earth with you. You may move in and out of each other's Heavens on Earth here and there, and there'll be times when many of you come together, all in your own experiences of Heaven on Earth, and together *you expand Heaven on Earth.*

Can you imagine one or two or three Heavens coming together? Imagine just for a moment. What if all of the planets, all of the places in the universe that have Heavens, really beautiful ones, came together for a *combined experience* of the highest Heavens in all of the universes and you got to experience them in form—you got to experience them as Heaven on Earth?

Think about it. You get to start merging all sorts of experiences of Heaven on Earth to expand yourself, to express yourself, to have new experiences, to live even more fully, and to love yourself *even more.* You can fulfill the divine plan through the expansion of Heaven on Earth. You can *fulfill your destiny* through the expansion of Heaven on Earth.

Some of you are really getting this. Some of you are really feeling it.

If you think of the explanation of anybody's vision of Heaven on Earth, it's light, beautiful, free, and fun. All those there are in peace and joy, living lovingly and harmoniously and creating and playing and having fun and dancing and singing and laughing. You know what it's like, even if you've never quite experienced it in form—*yet.* That seed was planted in your heart when *you focused yourself* into form. You placed that seed within you as you focused yourself into form.

That's why you know what it looks like. That's why you know what the vision is, and that's why you're here, and that's why you're remembering *now.* But your human self isn't going to figure it out. Your human self can't do it. Your human self can only *allow it.* It's not about training your human self, and it's not about untraining your human self. It's not about your human self really doing anything except allowing it to be done through you, being done *through* the physical form, but not through *any doing* from the human. Your human self will never figure it out.

Oh, we love your human forms so much. We do. We love your humans. You are expressing in these beautiful, beautiful personalities and bodies and expressions of form. But it's time to really let the God that you are express itself fully in this physical plane that you call *life*.

———

You can fulfill your destiny through the expansion of Heaven on Earth. It's time to let the God that you are express itself fully in this physical plane that you call *life*.

———

Your consciousness moves energy into form. You don't have to figure out what we mean. Your human doesn't have to figure it out, and in fact, they *can't* figure it out. It's your consciousness. It's your awareness. As you expand it—*not figure it out*, expand it, *not try to do it*, expand it—it moves energy into form, which means you have so much energy.

What does the energy do? It does everything. It does the thing that does everything, and it moves into form. Your consciousness and your awareness move energy, light, and power into form, which is manifestation, which is *creation*. That's the formula. That's the magic formula. That's the secret. That's the code. That's it. *That's the answer to your question right there, to every question.*

Consciousness moves energy into form. Consciousness and awareness move energy, move light into form, into creation, into manifestation. *That's it.* Nowhere does it say you have to dip down into lack or separation or struggle or sacrifice to move energy into form.

Consciousness moves energy into form. Consciousness, not specificness, not demanding, not even *praying*. Consciousness moves energy into form. All we're doing here while we're entertaining your magnificent brains is expanding the consciousness and expanding the awareness, which is what is moving the light and the energy into form. What is the form? Your creations, your manifestations, your destiny, the divine plan. It's moving it all into form. It's moving energy and light into the creation of Heaven on Earth. There's nothing to do. There's nothing to figure out. You don't need any answers. Consciousness and awareness move energy and light into form, into creation, into manifestation. And so it is.

We want to say one more thing about this because many of you still think that the purpose of all of this is to attract your soulmate or to win the lottery or to reverse aging in the physical body. It's not the purpose of any of this, although all of those things can happen. It's your expectation of them, the specific focus on them, that causes the resistance and the reaction, which limits the amount of energy that can move into form. When you understand that, you understand why certain things that you have wanted didn't happen. Your expectation, your specificness of it, created the resistance and the reaction of it not being present, which created the sensation of lack and separation, which limited the amount of energy and light, which cut it off from moving into form, which constricted the experience of form.

Your destiny is not *one* person. Your destiny is not *one* experience. Your destiny is not winning the lottery on a particular date. That's not your destiny. It might happen. Many of you will feel your relationships becoming more harmonious and easier and graceful and joyful, and you'll also notice that you're attracting people into your life who feel much more like-minded and aligned. You will feel that they are your soul family. You will feel a sense of destiny in your meetings, but your destiny is not just one person that you meet on one date. Your destiny is not just one day when a huge windfall of money lands in your lap. *That's not your destiny.*

Your destiny is not *one thing* you discover that creates a scientific advancement or a reversal in aging or a technological discovery. It's not that. Your destiny is that in every moment you're open and allowing and letting it flow, and in *every moment* you feel and know that *you're living your destiny*. It's the perfect allowing. Your destiny is for your human self to just allow it all in. That's your destiny. The specifics and expectations don't matter.

You're getting this. You're feeling this. You're stepping into Heaven on Earth. Then you think, *Well, I'm in Heaven on Earth. I think I should win the lottery, right? If I'm in Heaven on Earth, my soulmate must be here. If I'm in Heaven on Earth, I must be able to reverse my aging. If I'm in Heaven on Earth, I must be losing weight, right?*

And it's all fine and good. Yes, as you fully allow energy to move into form, you will have miraculous and magical experiences. But *destiny is the flow*. Destiny is the allowing. Destiny is *all of your experiences* being magical. Destiny is you living an extraordinary life experience. That's destiny. That's the divine plan *you created* for your life. And you did create it, we assure you.

———

Destiny is all of your experiences being magical.
Destiny is living an extraordinary life experience.

———

Take a breath, breathe it in, and let it go. Take another breath, breathe it in, and let it go. Take one more deep breath, breathe it in, and let it go.

Consciousness is what moves energy into form. Your awareness moves light into form. Your consciousness moves your energy and your light into Heaven on Earth.

Stay here in this consciousness, in this vibration, in this feeling, in this level of awareness. Perceive from *here*. Let your perspective come from *here*. Be here now. And so it is.

We love you so very much. We assure you something magical just happened. You just experienced your destiny. That's the greatest magic of all. You are, we assure you, the most beautiful thing you ever create. Creator within your own creation. Master of your life experience. The I Am That I Am Presence of All That Is. That is you. That is you, and that is why we are here for you. And so it is.

ESSENTIAL MESSAGES

- You have a clean slate now to never again experience the delay or the gap between you and your highest potential. It's better than you can imagine. It's better than you can ask for. This is our favorite part: *you're never going to figure it out.*

- There's other consciousness, there are other experiences, but there's nowhere that you are not because you are the light of the world.

- You are All That Is and all that will ever be. You are the highest good. You are the grandest potential. You are the greatest possibility. You are the most beautiful, magical, magnificent thing that you will ever create. You are the Source. You are the Divine. You are God. You are all of it.

- At this point, there's no way you could miss out on your destiny because of the level of awareness and consciousness that you are living in.

- As you start perceiving beyond the limitations of the physical senses, you start expanding your potential. You start expanding your possibilities. You allow a whole new reality to emerge through your perception of something *beyond.*

- Destiny is the flow. Destiny is the allowing. Destiny is all your experiences being magical. Destiny is you living an extraordinary life experience.

CHAPTER SEVEN

AWAKEN WITHIN THE DREAM

In this chapter, The Council challenges the human perception of what is real, helps lay the foundation for new paradigms, and invites you to live a life of pure magic.

We are so pleased and delighted to be here with each and every one of you in this time, in this place, in this sacred energy of All That Is, as you allow yourself to fully know yourself as the Source of All That Is—expressing yourself in the world for the fulfillment, enjoyment, and pure delight of your soul. We assure you that you are here to delight in this human experience and all that is here for you. *Aren't you starting to notice the pure magic that presents itself to you every day?* It just gets better. It just expands. There's just more. We assure you.

Your lives are an expression of *pure magic.* You are the expression of pure magic in the world. We assure you, every day, *every day* is a new opportunity to allow yourself to live in the miraculous and magical world that is here for you.

Heaven on Earth is becoming more real every day for each and every one of you, and in experiencing your own Heaven on Earth in your life you are bringing forth a new world, a New Earth, a better and more miraculous experience for any and all of those who are ready. And many *are* ready. You are going to see the Great Awakening expand like never before. You're going to see people in your families whom you never thought would fully awaken become conscious and aware of All That Is in a way that may surprise and delight you. You're going to see your family members, your friends, your co-workers, and your communities begin to awaken like never before to the power within, to the *more* that is going on here, to the divine plan that is expressing itself through you all. That is indeed why you have gone through your own miraculous transformation in the past 10 years.

Haven't you seen it really expedited in the past year? Aren't you *really* starting to see the quickening in your own life as the energy opens? As your awareness opens, as you allow yourself to receive, you are literally taking a quantum leap into an opportunity to live in Heaven on Earth that has *never* been present like it is right here, right now, because of the collective consciousness that *all* of you have reached, because of the vibration that you're able to maintain for long periods of time, and because of the level of awareness that you are existing in.

You are the existence of the Source itself in form. You are the very *existence* of All That Is here and now expressing yourself in the world. We will say you are needed more than ever before but not to fix the broken world, not to save others, not to drag them all to the finish line because you know the way or *think* you know the way. Let *them* walk their path just as you have, and let the magic and the miracles present themselves to them just as they have for you. Let them be guided and supported and assisted along the way just as you were and just as you are *every step of the way.*

Do not become the Source for others. Rather, stand in your power, the Source of All That Is that is *you* here and now. Shine your light brighter than you ever have before because you know who you are, you know how important you are, and you *know* that this is the time that you have been preparing for. This is why you're here, this is why you came, and this is why we say this is the best thing going on anywhere because indeed it is, here and now. You are part of it, and you are the expression of the divine plan in form.

Do not become the Source for others; stand in your power and shine your light brighter than ever before.

We have said it is time for you to awaken from the dream within the dream. Just as you awaken every morning and begin to move into the physical life experience and out of the dreamworld, let yourself move out of the physical life experience and into the dreamworld just as easily—with no resistance, with no hesitation, with no fear—because which is the real dream? Which part of it is real?

Think about it. When you are asleep at night, you are having experiences. You are expressing yourself. You are having interactions. You are moving through events and experiences and form that is much more fluid. It's a much more fluid experience of form. You can move in and out of things. You see things. You experience things. You get information. You get messages. You play things out. So, is that the dream? Or is *this* the dream? You move into this experience, and it's a little more dense. It *appears as if* things are solid and a little less fluid. It appears as if they're a little more real, but are they? Are they *really*?

Whatever you think is going on here in this human experience, whatever you think is missing, whatever you think isn't here yet, we assure you that you wouldn't even have the awareness of wondering why it's not in physical form if it wasn't already in your field. We assure you—it is. Could it be just as fulfilling to experience the full manifestation and creation and realization of everything you could ever want and more in what you might call a dream space, or is it really, really important to you that it take physical form for you to consider it real?

Which part is real? It's all really just a dream. It's all an opportunity for you to awaken within the dream and live as the Creator of your life experience in *all* dimensions of consciousness that you exist in, at all times. We assure you, you do exist in many dimensions of consciousness. However, you're focused on the human experience. There's so much for you in that experience, yes, but many of you are asking for more. *What is my real potential? What is my highest potential? What is really, really possible?*

The most important answer we can give you at this time is for you to awaken from the dream where there is suffering. Awaken from the dream—or the nightmare, you might call it—where there is suffering, where there is struggle, where there is death, where there is pain, where there is worry. All of that is just a playing out in a dream state of a deep subconscious story that you have about what this human experience is really about.

You are indeed entering into another significant phase of the Great Awakening. You have been preparing for this all your life, but most specifically in the past 10 years or so. As we have said, you are noticing a quickening of your own awakening, ascension, or expansion into living in higher dimensions of consciousness and awareness, which is possible through your elevated frequency and vibration—and being able to maintain it for longer periods of time.

There was a reason for all of it. Of course you have a choice. Of course you have free will. Of course you have the ability to go left or right at any moment. But as we have said, while you maintain free will in this human experience (and you always have, and you always will), when you live so aligned with your truth, with your soul, with your spirit, with your purpose, certain moments that present themselves to you are just choiceless. Now, we would agree they are *choiceful*, meaning there's no scarcity or lack. You're just so certain and so clear and so confident, but you're also so certain and so clear and so confident that you don't need to manipulate it or control it or push it or make it happen or force it.

You can allow it, and you can allow the moment where it's so clear to you that you have already sort of made the choice before you even have to make the choice. *That is part of allowing energy to serve you.* You have a potential or possibility that presents itself to you, and before long you're already down the path that has lit up for you. You just followed the energy, and there was never really a moment of making any sort of difficult choice. There was no trauma, there was no drama, there was no suffering, and there was no struggle because you never had to drag it down into limitation in order to move forward on your path with a knowing of what was in your highest and best good.

When you are allowing energy to serve you, things become so clear that you never have to make any difficult choices.

For much of your life you have sifted through different things to try to figure out what was right for you or what felt aligned with you, but oftentimes you had to move into struggle or suffering or density to get clear on what you really wanted. You can transcend that experience in form here, now, forevermore, if it is your choosing. But the important piece of that is to understand the role that energy plays.

You can use the word *energy*, or you can use the word *light*. Either way, start really being aware that, in opening and allowing energy, the path lights up for you, and you know this with certainty because you're already moving in that direction. You're staying in the flow and following the energy. Then there are not many times when you have to make a big decision, because the energy shows you the way, and you just allow it to flow because you are open, you are allowing and receiving. And what do we say about receiving? What is it that you are receiving? *Energy. Everything is energy.*

What do you want to receive? What do you want? *I want a loved one. I want a soulmate. I want someone to experience life with.* They are energy. That's what they are. The essence of what they are is energy. You want their *energy* in your life. You want the energy that flows through them in your life. You want how energy expresses itself through *them* in your life. That's why you want a particular person or a partner or a playmate.

If you want money . . . we've said all along, money is energy. It's just energy. *You've just created money as a form to barter your energy.* That's what it is. It's a form. It's energy that takes form to barter or exchange for more energy or for the balance of energy. It's energy. And if you want healing, if you want better health, if you want well-being, it comes from energy. It comes from opening and allowing energy. Energy does it all.

When we say *open and allow* and *receive* all that is here for you, you're receiving the energy. If you are not overly specific and so attached to what form it takes (because you already know that the creation has occurred), maybe it's in more of a liquid form, like a dream space. If you start experiencing it there, then you will live in such total integrity with energy, in such alignment to the flow, that you will transcend your *entire* human experience out of the lower-level, denser emotions, and you will live in a life experience as if it is a dream because there will be no struggle.

Your dreams are magical. Your dreams are beautiful. They are brighter than ever before. They are more vivid. They are more fluid, more magical. That's what your life experiences can be. As you allow that, you will find yourself living in an experience of Heaven on Earth that you always knew was your highest potential.

It's important that this is coming up. It's important that we're talking about it. It's important that you begin to transcend suffering because, as we have said, when you put suffering out of *your* human experience, you seed human consciousness with the potential to put suffering out of the *entire human collective experience.* When you put fear out of *your* experience, you just might make it possible for it to be transcended in the entire human experience. That's why you're the wayshowers. That's why you're the trailblazers. That's why you're the pioneers. That's why you're on the leading edge. *You are setting the vision into motion. You are laying the groundwork. You are creating new paradigms.*

Don't you want those new paradigms to be of the highest potential? Don't you want them to be pure and impeccable and beautiful and magical? You don't want these new paradigms to be latent with fear and struggle and suffering and worry, do you?

That would just be the old paradigm. This is not about changing the old paradigm. It's about creating new ones. This is not about creating some better way to wade through the river. It is about building a bridge to a better way, to a potential beyond suffering and struggle and fear and the experience of limitation.

You are the existence of the Source in physical form. You are the existence of God in form, expressing yourself as form. You are in form, *and* a grander part of you is not in any way limited to this form. When your human self understands that it is what creates limitation, then you can realize the work that you do as humans, the real difficult work, is holding yourself in the limitation that you yourself have created. You hold yourself in the limitation that you created for yourself. That's the density. That's the struggle. That's what takes a lot of work and effort. That's what's heavy. That's what breaks down the human body. That's what shuts you down from being open and allowing your energy to serve you in its highest form.

As you begin to be aware of the Great Awakening that is moving into the next phase, and you start noticing that many others are beginning to awaken around you, turn your light on *really bright*. Don't try to fix them. Don't try to save them. That's when it's most important for you to step fully into opening and allowing and receiving and living in *your own* experience of Heaven on Earth. You will notice that it is so much easier for them to find their way into higher dimensions of consciousness just by being in your presence when you are in higher states of consciousness yourself. You will not only begin to see magic presenting itself to *you* in ways it never has before, but you will also see magic going on in the world around you in a way that you never have before.

Living a miraculous life is not doing the impossible. Magical thinking is not trying to do the impossible. It's *redefining* what is possible for you. Only you can define through your own perception how you view life. Only you can define what's possible for you. Only you can really define what your highest potential is, what the highest possibility is for you. When you can hold that space, when you can hold your consciousness and your awareness at *that level*, allowing energy to flow through you—opening, allowing, receiving—and not being attached or specific about the form, you will find yourself redefining possibility, oh, in a way that you never really have imagined yet. And yet, you imagining it is what will move it into form.

**Magical, miraculous living is about
redefining what is possible for you.**

But again we say, if you can *enjoy* the fluid form of creation, you will not limit the physical expression of energy in form because what you still think is what you want or need is based on limitation. You're just scratching the surface of moving beyond your creations that come from lack and limitation.

You're going to move quickly. Things are going to pick up. You're going to feel quantum leaps forward. You're going to witness shifts in your own life that happen with absolute ease and grace and that are *truly* magical. You will have *no other explanation than that it was just pure magic* because you were redefining possibility and not getting stuck in expectation or specificness in a way that would limit your creation. Holding your consciousness and awareness at the highest level, opening and allowing energy, moves the grandest potential and possibility for you into form.

Any and all of this is only possible when you have an *unwavering* trust in the universe's expression through you being of the highest good always, and an unwavering trust in yourself and in your own *purity*, in your own *innocence*, and in yourself as an impeccable Creator within your own creation. All of that comes from an alignment to the I Am Creator frequency. Not the I-am-creating-a-healthier-body-and-reversing-aging frequency. Not an I-am-creating-more-money-because-I-can't-pay-this-or-that frequency. Not an I-am-healing-this-body-because-something's-wrong-with-it-and-this-has-been-going-on-for-a-really-long-time frequency.

Do you feel the difference? We say that jokingly, of course, but that's sort of why you think sometimes the universe isn't responding to you with *all* of its power, with *all* of its glory, with *all* of its magnificence when you are the one trying to control a situation or putting such specific expectation on form that you *limit* your own I Am Creator frequency. In doing that, you limit the amount of energy that flows through, so sometimes it doesn't feel like the universe is aware of you, responding to you, or knows where you are and sees the shortest path from where you are to your absolute highest potential and the greatest expression of all that you are in form.

We go back to understanding the example of your force field, of you being the center of the universe. Not because it's all about you and whatever you want, about you having more of this and more of that and having everything that you think you want and need from a limited human perspective. That's not what we mean when we say you're the center of the universe. There's not *one* of you that doesn't have a deep desire to contribute and make this world a better place. There's not one of you who doesn't love and care and have deep compassion for others and for the animals and for the planet and for all existence in the universe. You truly do, or you wouldn't be here.

We know you do, and we want you to remember that you *are* a force field of light and energy and creation expressing itself in form. *You, yourself, are a force field of creation.* You are a force field of creation expressing yourself in form, and the more you can allow yourself to be in the pure energy of the I Am Creator frequency, the more you will *allow* the future to come to you. You will *allow* miracles to present themselves to you. You will *allow* your life to be *pure magic*.

We know that there are some specific desires that you have. We always say to you that if there's something you really, really, really feel you need to experience in form, there's nothing wrong with that. It will serve you, and it will lead you to greater expansion and expression, and ultimately every experience you have will always lead you back to *you*.

You really can't get it wrong. You really can't get off the path. You really can't miss out. However, oftentimes when you get those things, there's a moment where you recognize the manifestation of it, but the moment it moves into form it starts to feel almost limited to you. You are the one who said, *I want it in form*, and now you are the one who says, *But now it feels limited because it is in form*. Interesting, huh?

You can allow yourself to experience yourself as Creator within your own creation, even if the creation feels a bit like a fluid dream space or imagination. Let it be just as enjoyable there as it would be if it were in form. When it comes into form, allow it the same dreamlike fluidity of expression and you will close the gap. Your creations will not feel limiting or as if they have moved into some form of density in order for you to enjoy and experience the fullness of them.

——

Allow your creations to maintain a dreamlike fluidity in form, and you will enjoy them in their fullness without density or limitation.

——

We love you all so much, and we say this with love and absolute understanding, but you entangle yourself in a lot of expectation, agreements, contracts, and commitments that you make in your life. You've made most of them never having really expected that you would get to this level of consciousness and awareness and freedom and energy and understanding of yourself as Creator. So you now have what you call *responsibilities*.

As you continue to elevate your consciousness and awareness, as you continue to maintain higher frequencies and vibrations, allowing more and more light and energy through you, you're going to expand at rapid rates into higher expression, higher experiences, more abundance, more joy, more peace, more harmony, more love, more openness. As you find yourself living in those places—which we would describe to you as your own Heaven on Earth—and as you start coming together and your Heaven on Earth begins to merge into an even more expanded experience, you might start feeling much more aware of limitation, and some of the things you feel responsible for might start feeling like they're limiting you. You'll *want* to change those people or the circumstances or the agreement. You'll want to go down into the layer where the form has taken place but now feels limiting.

We understand why that would be, but we also remind you that there is an easier, more effortless way. This is yet another example of you *not needing* to go down into lower, denser dimensions or lower, denser emotions to continue expanding your own experience of Heaven on Earth. The simple answer to *how* you do this is, first off, to not entangle or judge yourself or anyone else. *Your judgment will entangle you.* Your judgment of yourself will entangle you. Your judgment of others will entangle you. Your judgment of situations and circumstances will entangle you.

It's okay when that happens. Just notice it. The way you get yourself untangled is to move back into the moment, back into the present conscious moment, back to your awareness in this moment here and now, and align with a feeling of being totally satiated here and now, feeling into pure bliss, feeling into the magic of the moment, and then *expanding from there.*

Come back into the present moment. Go back into your heart. Come back into you. Come back into your force field instead of going out there and trying to hammer and chisel away at someone else's force field to get them to do what you want so that you can have what you think you need. Come back to you. Come back to the moment. Come back to the present now. Come back *home.* Come back home to you here and now. You. Your Heaven on Earth. *Come back home.* Come back into your dream. Come back into this moment. Come back into Heaven on Earth. Come back home and be here and be here now and feel totally satiated again.

Fill yourself up. Fill up the moment. Fill up the space. Fill up this home that is you with love and peace and joy and harmony and beauty. Fill up *your* force field again. Fill *your* home with love. Build your moment with the presence of all that you are, and then expand from here. Expand this moment. Expand the space around you. Expand your field. *Oh, that feels good.*

Then from this place of being fully open and allowing, feeling totally satiated in the moment, let the path light up. Let yourself be in the flow. Let the light show you the way. Let the energy gently guide you toward the next perfect step. Let the next perfect step come to you. Let the future come to you. Let the miracles present themselves to you. *Let yourself live in the magic again.* Then you're here, you're home. You're back here and now, and you're here. Just notice now that you're *here*, there's no struggle. Now that you're here, there's no fear. Now that you're here, there's no suffering because you're here. You're home. You're here. Be here now.

As you do this and you practice it and you're aware of it, you will begin to create from your alignment to this energy here, the I Am Creator frequency. You will create within your own creation, within your own field, within your own energy, within the flow, *within Heaven on Earth.* You begin to create, the Creator within your own creation, with no agenda. True creation has no agenda. No agenda, no expectation, and no limitation, which means no struggle, no suffering, no sacrifice, no fear, no worry. Just pure, innocent, impeccable creation with effortless ease that will move into form in the easiest, most harmonious way, *the highest expression of creation within your own experience.*

———

Pure creation moves into form in the easiest, most effortless, most harmonious way.

———

When you can balance *that* level of existence and experience— while also letting everyone else have their own experiences and choose for themselves—and maintain your I Am Creator frequency in the world at this time of the next phase of the Great Awakening, you will see many, many more people, like never before, *eager and excited to transcend the old and to move into the new with you.* But this is not about fixing the old world.

We say that the Fifth Dimension, the New Earth, Heaven on Earth is not a different place. It is a different state of consciousness, but in that different state of consciousness, new realities are created. Within those *new* realities that are created, *new* form takes place, and consciousness moves energy into form in a new way, in a more expanded way. For metaphorical purposes, if you were to imagine that there was a New Earth in parallel and in perfect motion to Old Earth, if you want to call it that, then you are either in the New Earth or you are in the Old Earth. You have to choose where you are. You can only be in one place at one time.

So, you're either choosing the New Earth—Heaven on Earth—or you're choosing the Old Earth. In the New Earth, there is peace and joy and love and harmony and beauty and collaboration and cooperation at the highest level. There's co-creation at the highest level. There is a merging of multiple different expressions of Heaven on Earth coming together in their purest form from absolute innocence, and all beings that live in that New Earth are *impeccable Creators*.

And then there's the Old Earth. There's nothing wrong with it. It's not a comparison, but the Old Earth still has polarity, has density, has experiences of separation, experiences of lack and struggle and pushing and efforting and trying to move *form* in order to get it the way you want it. There are all the things that you don't really like so much, which is why you've been doing all this work on yourself in the first place—to transcend fear, struggle, suffering, lack, and limitation. Then you get to the place where you know you *can*, and you still choose to live in Old Earth.

There's nothing wrong with this. We just want you to see it in a visualization. We want you to be able to picture the difference so that you know what you're choosing energetically. You all are here to help create the New Earth, to move it into form and then have the experience of it. Then you say, *But wait, don't I have to still change the whole Old Earth in order for me to live in the New Earth?* And we say, *No, you actually can't.* That's not the way it ever could be.

Think about it as an undiscovered fishing spot. There's a beautiful lake, and somewhere special in the middle of the lake is this sacred spot where there is an absolute abundance of fish, and there's never a limited supply, *ever*. They're the most beautiful fish, and there's an ease to finding the fish in that spot. It's a magical fishing spot. It can be raining on the other side of the lake, but when you go to that spot in the lake it's sunny and beautiful. Anytime you're ever there and someone else is also fishing in that spot, it doesn't change your experience.

Your experience is still wonderful even if someone else is there fishing in the same spot, and you notice that every time someone else is also fishing in that sacred fishing spot, you really like them. They're amazing. They're fun. They're funny. They get you. You connect. You have great conversations as you're fishing. More and more people start coming to this fishing spot, but every time there's no limitation on how many fish *you* have. *There's just always an abundance.* Everyone you meet there is incredible, and you start really loving the sacred fishing spot. There's no lack. There's no limitation to how many people can be there, and every time you meet someone there it seems to add something to your life. It seems to just get better and just get bigger, and together it sort of seems like you all have more, a better life, a more magical life, and there's just an abundance of life.

Would you ever want to go back to the experience of struggle and difficulty and chaos, or would you just enjoy your new fishing spot? Would you ever go back and fish at a fishing hole where there are never any fish, the weather is always crappy, and if somebody else goes there, they're kind of a jerk? No, you would choose to fish at the new fishing spot.

You can *choose* where you want to be. *It's that simple.* Think about it this way. If all of a sudden everybody chose to live in the New Earth, wouldn't there just be more? Wouldn't it just be better? And if only half the people decided to live there and the other half decided to live in the Old Earth, well, that's okay too, right? Lastly, if only just a few people decided to live in the New Earth but lots decided to stay in the Old Earth, that's also fine.

You can choose whether you want to live in the New Earth or the Old Earth. It's that simple.

Here's the second part of the story. Now you're a soul, and you're coming into the Earth experience, and you get to choose. *Well, do I want to come to Earth in the New Earth or the Old Earth?* If you are in the New Earth and you know that every soul has that choice when they come into this experience, you realize that some chose to go to Old Earth. And you think: *I don't know why. I don't want to presume why. I honor them. I know the truth of them. I don't need to know why they chose the Old Earth. I can choose to live in the New Earth. I know that they came with a soul, with a choice just as I did, and I'm never going to figure out why they chose to go to Old Earth or why they chose to stay there when at any time they could have come to the New Earth.*

I know who they are. I know the truth of who they are, so I'm going to let them have their experience. I'm not going to go into the Old Earth and try to fix them or save them because I know they have a choice, just like I do. They can come swim and fish and play in the magical fishing spot because there's more than enough. There's a plentiful supply. There's an abundance of all the good things.

You get to choose for you, and everybody else gets to choose for them. Let it be. Let it be their experience. It doesn't have to affect what you choose for you. As you redefine what's possible in your life experience, you make it easier for so many others to choose a more magical experience for themselves. That's how important you are.

You are here seeding human consciousness with a greater potential and possibility. You are illuminating the potential for humankind. You are free to live the life you choose for you where you can allow all things with ease and grace. *Let the light guide the way*, and you will dance and play with the beauty of all of creation. You *are* the existence of All That Is, here and now, the

Creator within your own creation. *Come home to you.* Wake up from the dream, and wake up to you. *Wake up to you.*

Every single one of you is so magnificent in every way, and all that's left to do is allow and open and receive. *I allow all that I am, I allow all that I am, I allow all that I am, and so it is.* In the opening and the allowing yourself to transcend into a new, more glorious dream, you illuminate the potential for all of humankind. Allow every day, every moment to be a bright new glorious morning for you. It is all here for you *now.* You will enjoy, you will delight in being in this experience, fully home to you—coming back to you, yourself, within your own field and moving through life from *this* place as you witness *not only your own shift in consciousness* to redefine what's possible, but also see the Great Awakening taking place on your planet at this time, *awakening everyone to the potential to choose the world you want to live in.* Only you can choose for you. And so it is.

—

Allow every day, every moment to be a bright new glorious morning for you. It is all here for you now.

—

We know we have brought a lot to you. Let this be an expansion of your consciousness and awareness. Let this be an elevation of your light and your frequency. Notice that you are maintaining these higher vibrations for longer and longer periods of time as you expand your consciousness and your awareness. As you do, you open up and allow more energy and light, which moves you *even more powerfully* into yourself as Creator within your own creation.

So, take a deep breath, and let it go. Take a deep breath, and let it go. One more time. Take a deep breath, and *let it go.* And so it is.

ESSENTIAL MESSAGES

- You're going to see people in your families who you never thought would fully awaken become conscious and aware of All That Is in a way that may surprise and delight you.

- It's all really just a dream, and it's all an opportunity for you to awaken within the dream and live as Creator of your life experience in all dimensions of consciousness that you exist in, at all times.

- You are a force field of creation. The more you can allow yourself to be in the pure energy of the I Am Creator frequency, the more you will *allow* the future to come to you. You will *allow* miracles to present themselves to you. You will *allow* your life to be *pure magic*.

- If you can enjoy the fluid form of creation, you will not limit the physical expression of energy in form.

- The Fifth Dimension, the New Earth, Heaven on Earth is not a different place. It is a different state of consciousness.

- As you redefine what's possible in your life experience, you make it easier for so many others to choose a more magical experience for themselves.

CHAPTER EIGHT

LET THE LIGHT GUIDE THE WAY

In this chapter, The Council invites you to recognize the existence of God in all things and to remember that the energy is always guiding you, showing you the way.

We are so pleased and delighted to have the opportunity to speak with you all on this fine and glorious day indeed. You are divine beings of light expressing yourself in the world for your enjoyment and pure delight. You are everything you wish to be. You are free. You are free. You are All That Is expressing yourself in form. Remember that life is meant to unfold for you with ease and grace in the most *magnificent* ways.

You are coming to a time where there is an acceleration happening. Many of you are feeling it as a bit of resistance, many of you are feeling it with heightened emotions, and many of you are feeling it with a greater sense of experiencing the void than you have before. There is an acceleration. There is a quickening. There's a speeding up. We offer you an invitation to experience this acceleration with grace; grace being the allowing of light, allowing of the existence of the Divine, allowing of yourself—the divine being that you are—to *be* in a state of allowing, allowing, allowing.

What are you allowing? Energy. You're allowing energy. You are allowing light. When you start understanding that the acceleration and the quickening is happening as a result of *your* asking, *your* expansion, *your* ability to hold yourself in a higher frequency for longer periods of time, you will realize that it is more important than ever before to practice being impeccable.

We have said that *impeccable* means "in the highest good, of the highest standards." Your human definition even states that being impeccable means not liable to sin. What does that mean? Some of these words have a great amount of energy around them, like the word *sin*. At times they have been used to control, judge, and shame people. Yet all that was ever meant in the intention of the word *sin* was to miss the mark, to miss the higher meaning, to miss the higher potential.

So then, impeccable means not liable to miss the higher intention, the higher purpose, the higher good. That there's something grander available, some greater potential, some higher possibility. If you will allow creation to be impeccable, you will find that there's a higher good involved in it all that your human self cannot see, cannot figure out, and will never understand. If you're viewing life experiences and what is happening around you as *bad* or *good*, you tend to move into a state of judgment, which tends to move you into limitation. It tends to have you looking at whether creations are right or wrong, whether manifestations are right or wrong, whether people are right or wrong, or whether situations are right or wrong, and you tend to miss the mark, miss the target, miss the point, which is that everything, *everything* is the expression of God. It is your perception that determines how you experience God in reality. Oh, we've never said that before. It's really important.

———

Everything is the expression of God, and your perception of your life experience determines how you experience God in reality.

———

Everything is the existence of the Divine. Everything is the existence of God, of the Source. It could be no other way, but most of the time you are denying the existence of God in everything because of your judgment of what is right and what is wrong. You deny yourself as the power that you are, as the force field, as the very existence of creation that is you. You are the existence of creation. You are creation. You are reality. But your perception of God is what determines your experience of reality. The more you allow the power that you are, the more expansive your life becomes, the more you see the beauty in all things, the more you see and experience and feel God, the more you witness the Divine in your human experience.

You deny yourself by shaming yourself, by judging yourself, by blaming yourself, by holding yourself in guilt and resentment. We have spoken many times about shame being the heaviest, densest human emotion, and many of you have become very aware of when you shame yourself. Now you are moving toward a process of moving beyond, going beyond, transcending judgment, and seeing how it entangles you with lower-dimensional energies and emotions. It is your denying—through your judgment of others, of yourself, of situations—that keeps you from experiencing the Divine, keeps you from Heaven on Earth, keeps you from experiencing the creation of all that exists in your force field.

Many of you think you still need to be clear on or be specific about what you want to manifest, and we are telling you it's all already in your force field of creation, and if you just don't go into the gap, you will experience the fullness of all that is here for you now. But you cannot experience the fullness of all that you are, all that life has to offer in every situation, and all who you are co-creating with if you are denying, through your judgment, the very existence of the Source that is everywhere, the Divine that is in everything.

You deny the very Source that you are, the divine being that you are, through your judgment of yourself. Every time you resist something because you feel you didn't do it right, you judge it as wrong. You judge emotions as wrong. We have never, ever said that feeling lower, denser emotions is *wrong*. We've never said it's wrong. It's not wrong. Is it your highest potential? Is it the highest possibility? Is it the fullness of all that you are? Maybe not, but it's not *wrong*. There's data and information in all of it.

You are here reading our words. You drew us to you because you remember somewhere within you that life is meant to be easy, effortless, and harmonious, that grace and energy and light are available to you at all times, that your life is meant to be joyful, that this journey is meant to be *enjoyed*, and that you are here to enjoy and delight in all that you are. That's why you drew us to you.

It is your asking that is drawing to you an awareness to shift beyond lower, denser emotion. This awareness is coming to you because you are asking to transcend these lower, denser energies, but not because we've ever said they're wrong. Your very awareness of the ability to shift into some other wanted place is a highly conscious, enlightened state of being. Why would you judge yourself for being conscious and aware of your state or of how you feel?

———

**Feeling lower, denser emotions is not wrong.
Your very awareness of the ability to
shift into a wanted place is a highly
conscious, enlightened state of being.**

———

You are *feeling* beings, and the truth will come to you through your feelings. That is your mechanism that guides you. How does it *feel*? Oftentimes what trips you up about this is where you think you *should* be or what you *should* be doing or what you *should* feel instead of staying conscious and present and witnessing what it is that this feeling is showing you. It's usually showing you that you're holding yourself in limitation through the way that you're thinking, through your choices, your actions, your perception. That is all.

Why do you deny the existence of God in others? Why do you deny the existence of God in yourself? Why do you deny the existence of God in all situations? Because you really want certain things to be right, and you really want certain things to be wrong—because then you'll have control. Is that *really* what you want, control of all of this? The second you try to control everything, you yourself will feel out of control.

You sometimes have situations in your human experience, such as the spread of a virus, fluctuating financial markets, economic turbulence, wars between nations or political leaders, natural disasters, crime, and threats of violence that appear to be the reason many people feel out of control. It is a common belief under such circumstances that the way to get it under control is to figure out how to manipulate that particular thing or experience. In these types of situations you are playing out perceived limitations and trying to control things, because if you have control then you will be *safe*. It's just a state of awareness or a misunderstanding of your ability to navigate the human experience with ease and grace. For example, you may think that if something was deemed as safe by your governments or an authority figure, then you wouldn't have to check in with your own navigation systems. You don't have to follow the energy and light that are always guiding you if something outside of you is telling you what's safe, where to go, and what you can and can't do in order to stay safe and keep everything under control.

This will lead you back to remembering that when you allow the light to guide the way, there's no need to control. When you allow energy to guide the way for you, there's no need to control. There's nothing out of control, and it's not by getting things "under control" that you feel better. It's by moving into a state of *allowing*, which means to take a deep breath, slow down, connect to all of you, expand the space around you, open and allow energy to serve you, and then follow the light, follow the energy, and go with the flow. Not the flow of what the masses are doing or thinking or feeling. Flowing with the light, flowing with the energy. The flow of the light and the energy will guide you *always*.

The *situation* of something like a virus, natural disasters, violence, or war is no different than any other situation. People make their transitions—or what you call death—every day through a wide variety of means, some of which have been around for a long time, and yet where do you feel out of control? Where do you feel the need to control in order to be safe? Whenever you're feeling a need to control, you're just moving yourself out of the state of allowing energy and light to guide the way.

Why do you deny the existence of God in others? Because you really want them to stay under control. Why do you deny the existence of God in certain situations? Because you want to control the situation to be the way you think it should be from your limited vantage point or viewpoint. We assure you, there is a much higher, grander perspective in *all* situations.

———

You deny the existence of God in things because you want to control them from your limited viewpoint.

———

You look at a situation like a hurricane, and you think, *That's awful. That's terrible. It shouldn't be that way; it's out of control, causing devastation.* And you go into fear and mass conscious dis-ease and in some cases insanity because it's just out of control. But *you* don't have to ever be out of control. When you don't need to control, there is ease.

Consider how you use the very word *control*. It's under control. It's locked down. It's put in its box, in its place. It's under control. It's moved into such a form of density that it has no ability to harm you. You deny the existence of God that is in all things and everyone, because if everyone knew the power within them, then the situation would just be out of control. That's the common way of thinking, which holds you in lack and limitation, in the feeling of being out of control and needing to control, in the feeling of being unsafe, and in getting entangled in lower-density emotions and mass conscious thinking.

As it relates to any sort of situation that is unwanted, in every moment there is the ability to tune into, open, and allow energy to serve you, and to let the light guide the way. This means you might be guided around doing something that you do every single day because there is something in your path that day that is not a vibrational match to you; it's not in your field, because it's not in the highest and best good, and not aligned with your experience of creation. Yet you often move into your unconscious response to the day-to-day without staying present.

One of our dear friends illustrated this perfectly. We have asked you, *What brings you joy? Do that. What brings you joy? Do that. What brings you joy? Do that.* She likes to walk on a particular trail every day, and that has brought her joy, so she walks along it on many days. She has a path she likes to take, so she takes that path because that's the path she likes, that's the path that brings her joy. On one particular day, she had energy light up and tell her to go a different way, but she's so used to her joy coming from going in the other direction that she didn't follow the light. She didn't follow the energy, and there's no judgment from our side ever.

We have so much love for our friend, and yet so much can be learned and remembered from her experience. There was a somewhat aggressive dog on the path she normally follows, and light was guiding her another way. Instead of avoiding that dog, she came across it, but in shifting fairly quickly back into her heart, she was able to avoid an unwanted situation, and all was essentially well. But was the whole situation guided and orchestrated as such that everyone reading this message could reach an understanding of how to follow the energy and light that will *always* guide you around obstacles or things that are not aligned in your field? We think so.

Let's say that you are supposed to be at a meeting, and you are going to get on an airplane to get there, but it isn't coming together easily, effortlessly, harmoniously. There is no light in it. There is no energy in it. You don't feel any resonance at all, but you feel like you *have* to go to the meeting. So you go, and you end up catching the flu, or you end up being delayed, or you end up having a situation. *You would be more upset that you did not trust your own guidance system* than that you were delayed or that you got the flu.

Now, we agree that it's possible for every single one of you to live in perfect health at all times if you are willing to slow down, put some space around yourself, stay in the light, and let the light guide the way—meaning to stay in a high frequency, a high vibration, in a state more aligned toward being totally satiated and feeling pure bliss and peace and ease and joy and in a state of grace. Your body will naturally, naturally stay in the highest state of well-being. You may say, *But I have to do these things. I'm responsible for these things. I'm responsible for these people. I'm responsible for this job. I'm responsible for all these things I have to do.* When you say these things, you move out of your state of grace, and you find yourself being unwell.

The same is true in relationships. When one is fearful of entering into a relationship because they might get hurt or they don't fully allow themselves to be vulnerable, it's usually—and we'll say *always*—because you have had an experience of being in a relationship in the past where the energy went out of that relationship, where the light moved you somewhere else but you didn't go with the light. You stayed attached, dependent, in expectation that the relationship had to work, and you pushed, you struggled, you forced, and you got hurt, and they got hurt. Harm was caused not because you can't trust love, but because you didn't follow the energy, you didn't follow the light. When the light left the relationship, you didn't go with it. You held yourself in the dark.

Understand that you can navigate through *all* of life, including relationships, with ease and grace in the most effortless, harmonious way when you follow the energy. If you think of spending time with your loved one today and it doesn't bring a smile to your face, then let the energy guide the way. When you say, *I have to, they're my spouse,* or *I have to, they're my child,* or *I have to, my sister is in town,* then you are denying the energy. You're denying the light that's trying to guide you, and you're holding yourself in limitation because you think you *should,* because you feel *responsible.*

We are unearthing, uncovering, bringing to the light, bringing to your awareness something really important here. Some of you might really get it, and some of you might take some time to uncover and internalize it. You often know things with absolute certainty. You can call it intuition, or you can call it a feeling, but it's the energy. It's the light always guiding you. You wouldn't have agreed to come into this human experience if you didn't know with absolute certainty that the light would always, *always* guide the way for you. You knew you could feel whether the energy was in something or not, so you'd always know which way to go, which step to take, which path to follow, simply because you allowed the energy and you felt for the energy.

———

The light will always guide the way for you.
You can feel whether the energy is in something
or not, so you always know which way to go.

———

Some have come to a belief in limitation, which says you pick one person and you stay with them forever. We're not saying that it's not a very *real* experience for people to have loving, harmonious relationships. We're not saying that you should end a relationship because you didn't have a good day with them. However, times of struggle in any relationship occur when you deny the existence of God in yourself, in the other person, and in the situation.

When you can get back to allowing the *purity* that is in everything, the *possibility* that is in everything, the *power* that is in everything, you will align to the highest potential of any situation. You'll align to the highest possibility of any relationship. You will see the Divine in everyone, no matter who or what they appear to be in that moment, and you will allow yourself to be the fullness of all that you are. You will stay open and allowing, and you will find yourself navigating through life with ease and grace and harmony in all your relationships and situations.

It takes some slowing down at first. It takes creating space, and it gets easier. It does. All we're trying to do is bring this to the light for you so that you can experience more magic, more miracles, more experiences of divine orchestration, more ease and grace.

We don't use the word *choiceless* to imply that you don't have a choice. But really, if you think about it, you want it to feel choiceless. You want it to be clear and obvious and feel so aligned that there's absolute clarity, absolute confidence, absolute certainty, and that you just *know*. And you want to get really good at staying open and allowing. Even if the light and the energy is guiding you right where you are in this moment and nowhere else, *that is an action*. Sometimes the action is to be right where you are and to find the opportunity to be an even greater expression of the Source that you are here and now.

We understand that you *believe,* and you have learned through this human experience that there are things you *have* to do. You're coming into a time of really discovering a new level of limitation that you have agreed to and deciding from a more conscious, aware perspective whether you want to continue allowing that in your experience. The thing that will help you is to start being aware of the formless, unmanifested existence of creation—the formless reality, the unmanifested reality that is always available to you. *That is allowing yourself to experience All That Is in your force field of creation.*

Consider the very insightful observation that manifesting something often leads to feeling responsible for the thing you have manifested. If you want to experience having a child—being a portal by which life moves into form or a being moves into the human experience—and you manifest it, then you become responsible for the child for the rest of your life. All these responsibilities seem to come with it.

Perhaps you want to find your soulmate. You want to experience being with the love of your life. You want to find love. You want to attract a partner, and you want it *so badly* to be in form so that you can touch them and play with them and kiss them and laugh with them and do things with them and support each other. Then, suddenly, you have a whole new level of responsibility because of the manifestation of this lover in form.

The same is true with a business. Many of you want to leave your jobs and the experience of being employees to have your own businesses or services or work that you do. Yet in the manifestation of that comes a whole lot of responsibility. Now you're responsible for all these customers and all this work that needs to get done and all these things that must be taken care of.

There is an experience you have of wanting to manifest things and not wanting to move out of the cycle of creation into being responsible for them. When you understand that impeccable creation has no agenda, you can experience pure Source expressing through you. If it moves into form or manifestation, if it comes from purity and impeccable-ness and can exist more freely in form, you can navigate through the experience of form without imposing such limitation on your manifestation by judging what's right or wrong or denying the existence of God in your creations. This also means that you don't then manifest something and decide that you're the Source of it, that you are the all-knowing. When you're trying to control the manifestation—when you're trying to control *when* it manifests, *how* it manifests, *who* it manifests— then you start feeling this control over the manifestation, which makes you feel out of control, which is what causes a *great* amount of the trauma and the drama and the suffering in your creations.

———

You can navigate through the experience of form without imposing limitations on your manifestation.

———

When you are *controlling* creation, it's not really creation. When you are controlling manifestation, it almost always makes you feel out of control. You're out of control because it has not manifested, and then you're out of control because it *has* manifested. You're out of control when it hasn't manifested, because you're in lack and separation and in the gap, and you believe that if it would just manifest, the gap would be gone. But the truth is that you then create a *new* gap by your sense of responsibility for it. We have said that a great part of this experience is taking full and total responsibility for your life, which includes what you've created and what you've manifested and your choices and your actions and your behaviors. Then remember, truly, it's *not* that big of a deal. It's just not that big of a deal. It's not.

You are one of billions of beings having the human experience, living the human experience, in the human experience. All of you are creating all the time, and this has been going on for a long, long time and will continue to go on for a long, long time. There are lots of other beings and lots of other dimensions creating as well. It's endless, always, eternal, ever-present creation. So one simple choice that you made is not *that* big of a deal. One manifestation that you have experienced, no matter how big or little it seems, is really not that big of a deal. But how you perceive it determines the existence of God within it.

For example, you couldn't even count how many trees are on your planet! Yet every single one of them is a manifestation of creation, of the Source. The seed and soil and water and sunlight that created each tree are manifestations of the Source.

Now, there was no intelligence trying to control the tree as it was being created. There was no intelligence trying to control it. It was just the pure expression of the Source allowing the seed to become whatever it became. There are so many trees, you can't even count them, but from time to time don't you notice that you have a favorite tree, that there is this one tree that is your *favorite* tree? It's the most beautiful tree. It's the big, beautiful tree in your yard, or it's the bright, vibrant tree in the park, or it's the strong, sturdy, old tree in the forest. There are countless trees. They're all creation and the Source, but *it's your love of that one tree that makes it special*, that makes it holy, that makes it sacred.

You decide what is holy and sacred. *You decide* to experience the existence of the Divine. It's you. You're the one deciding the existence of the sacredness, the holiness, the divinity in *your reality*. Then you can decide that every tree is holy and sacred even though others could walk by the same trees and not see the existence of God anywhere. They'd think there was nothing special about those trees, that they're just trees. Yet you can decide that *that* tree is holy and sacred, that all the trees are, that the humans are, that the animals are, that the planet is. You can decide that the air you breathe is sacred. You can decide that the air you breathe is holy and divine. You can decide that the people in your life are sacred and holy and divine. *You can decide that you are.* You can choose, you can assume, you can decide to experience the existence of God and the Source in everything instead of denying it. And you do that by slowing down, creating space, being present, allowing all that you are.

———

You can decide to experience the existence of God and the Source in everything by slowing down, creating space, being present, allowing all that you are.

———

If you stood across from a tree, and you were looking at it, and you really allowed yourself to be in the moment, if you really sat in the moment in the fullness of all that *you are* and allowed the space around you to expand and allowed your force field to expand, you would begin to see the energy of the tree and that there was almost a liquid-like space around the tree. You would notice that it wasn't just air—there was something else. There is almost this liquid form around the tree, and you would start to see that form expand. You would start to see an energy around the tree. The tree would almost begin to light up, and you would notice the light within you and the field around you, and you would begin to notice that there's no place that the light is not in the tree or in you. *The light is between you, and it is you, and it's all around you and the tree.*

If you continued to stay in the presence and allowed the light and opened and allowed the energy, you would feel absolute oneness with the tree. You would tune in to all the knowledge and the wisdom and the consciousness, not only of that tree but of the entire system that is supporting the tree.

If you sat in that moment and really allowed it, you would experience God in yourself, in the tree, in everything that created it, in everything that created you. You would feel into it with such awareness that it was a *holy* experience, a *sacred* experience. It was ultimate creation, *ultimate creation* without any control, without any lack or separation, allowing the fullness of all that you are, allowing creation with ease and grace in the most expansive, beautiful, impeccable way.

That can be experienced with everything, with anything, with people, with yourself. In any situation there is an untapped expression of the Divine. A holy moment is always available to you. It's just a matter of whether you're perceiving the existence of God in your reality of All That Is.

If you want to experience more magic in your life, it starts by how you experience your life. Are you experiencing everything around you for the magic that it is? Magic, the unseen power, the unexplainable power, the existence of something beyond logic—it exists in everything.

This is a shifting of your perspective, a raising of your consciousness and awareness. We are here to expand the potential and possibilities for your life experience, and in that you yourself will illuminate the potential for humankind. You seed human consciousness with a new potential and possibility.

You're going to see an acceleration. You're going to see a quickening. Your ability to navigate that with ease and grace will be determined by how much control you exert on creation and reality and All That Is. If you are experiencing the acceleration and trying to control others, situations, and manifestation, you will create resistance and the feeling of being out of control. When you can allow creation without needing to control it because you totally trust your own ability to stay open and allow energy to light the way and guide the way, then you no longer need or want to control at all.

Just bringing this into your awareness will shift it for you, will make it easier. We bring it into your awareness because of your trajectory at this time, because of what is in your field and what is moving into your experience. The acceleration you asked for, the quickening you asked for, the up-leveling you asked for, the next level of creation you asked for, let it come. Let it come with ease and grace. Do not try to control it, or you will feel out of control.

Do not try to control it. Allow it. Allow yourself to be all that you are. Allow your reality to grow and expand. Allow yourself to express all that you are. Allow yourself to *live* fully in Heaven on Earth. Allow yourself to *love* fully. Allow yourself to be all that you are with no resistance, no control, no expectation, and no need to figure it all out, and you will feel one of the greatest shifts you've experienced in your life so far. You will literally see your *entire* reality up-leveling to a whole new state of existence and experience.

Allow yourself to be all that you are, and you will see your entire reality up-leveling to a whole new state.

Stay open, stay allowing, and let energy guide the way. Don't try to control it. When you feel out of control, the most important thing you can do is stop, take a breath, come back into the fullness of all that you are, put some space around yourself, feel your connection opening and allowing energy, move back into the light, move back into the awareness of the force field, let energy guide the way, and let the light guide the way. Then, you will navigate this incredible time in the most harmonious way. And so it is.

You really are in incredible, incredible times. We know it's not always easy, but it can continue to get easier, lighter, freer, more delightful, more enjoyable, more harmonious, more exciting. You are everything you wish to be. You already are. We truly honor you for who you are. *There is great love here for you always.*

ESSENTIAL MESSAGES

- Everything is the expression of God. It is your perception of it that determines how you experience God in reality.

- You're denying the light that's trying to guide you, and you're holding yourself in limitation because you think you *should*, because you feel *responsible*.

- When you can get back to allowing the purity, the possibility, and the power that is in everything, you will align to the highest potential of any situation.

- You want it to feel choiceless. You want it to just be clear and obvious and feel so aligned that there's absolute clarity, absolute confidence, absolute certainty, and that you just *know*.

- When you're trying to control the manifestation—when, how, who—you feel out of control, which causes a great amount of trauma, drama, and suffering in your creation.

- You can decide to experience the existence of God and the Source in everything by slowing down, creating space, being present, allowing all that you are.

CHAPTER NINE

NAVIGATING CURRENT EVENTS WITH PEACE AND GRACE

In this chapter, The Council shares a broader perspective of the transformation occurring on the planet and the importance of living consciously during this time of awakening.

We are so pleased and delighted to have the opportunity to speak with you all about important times when you are called to navigate through incredible transformations on *every level* that is visible to the human eye. Whether it is a very personal experience or some global event, there will be times when you encounter rapid change.

Look around at your planet and you will notice that you are seeing transformation moving itself into form at an unprecedented rate. You are seeing the Great Awakening of your human family. You are seeing the next phase of transformation and the elevation of human consciousness. No matter how it may appear at any time, this is not chaos. Nothing has gone wrong here. This is an opportunity. This is a response to a grander desire or intention, and an asking for balance, for consciousness, and for transformation.

We invite you first and foremost to remember that there is a grander plan. There is always more going on in your experience than you can see. If you will stay in a state of peace, if you will stay in a state of internal harmony and balance, you will be consciously guided—not only in navigating these times, but consciously guided in your awareness that more is going on here than may be understood by those around you or within the mass conscious collective. The experiences of your life and of your world are bringing balance on many levels.

For an example of navigating change while holding a grander perspective, let's consider the experience of a widespread virus. First, take the concept of viruses altogether, which in their very existence restore balance to systems. Viruses bring balance with an "out with the old, in with the new" sort of cleaning up of systems and making way for expansion, evolution, and a new environment to emerge.

If you are in such an experience, do not push against, do not go into resistance, and do not make the virus itself wrong. *It is not.* Do not choose and decide to go into judgment of good or bad or right or wrong and try to eliminate something that *you* believe from a limited human perspective is going wrong.

In that case, some of you may ask why we didn't prophesize or forecast these events in great detail. We are always preparing you for what is coming into your reality and providing you with wisdom and guidance to help you navigate through any experience more gracefully and more easily from a level of consciousness that is always available to you. We know that those of you who may ask that question would do so because you found yourself in fear, you found yourself in the chaos, you found yourself in resistance in the moment. From that state you would then ask us, *Why did you not tell us months ago?*

We say, because then you would have had the same reaction months ago. You would have had three months of fear, three months of resistance, three months of reaction instead of feeling those emotions just in the present moment. We also say that the next thing you would have thought is, *How do we prevent this? How do we get rid of this?* You would have gone into judgment that the foretold experience was bad. You would have gone into reaction and tried to eliminate it, tried to fight it. That is not what is asked of you in experiences of great change. What is asked of you more than ever is to stay conscious, stay present, practice all that you know, be in peace, and create an entire field of peace within and around your being.

———

**What is asked of you is to stay
conscious and to create an entire field of
peace within and around your being.**

———

There are *always* changes occurring in the field. No matter when you are reading this, change is always occurring. Change is always going to happen. We want you to get really good at navigating change with ease and grace and balance and harmony and peace and joy and an ability to hold a grander, higher perspective of whatever is happening around you, instead of going into mass conscious fear.

Whatever you are feeling in the moment is what you are contributing to human consciousness. If in this moment you are in fear, you are adding to the fear. If there is chaos within you at this moment, you are adding to the chaos. Not only are you adding to the mass conscious chaos and fear, you are stressing the body. You are creating resistance within your own body, which will then seek *balance.*

The greatest thing you can do is remember that anytime you are in resistance, you are causing pain to yourself. Any type of resistance creates pain—emotional, physical, mental. When you are in resistance or you are experiencing stress, you are adding a great amount of density and disease to the body, and imbalance occurs. The most important thing you can do is be in peace, breathe, smile, laugh, and be uplifted. You can absolutely choose to elevate yourself beyond any experience of imbalance. You can choose to elevate your consciousness beyond the dimension or the density of experience where the imbalance is occurring. You can *absolutely choose* to elevate your consciousness out of the experience or the dimension or the level of density where the imbalance is occurring.

If you elevate your consciousness and awareness, you will elevate your vibration, and your body will follow. You can *choose* not to participate in fear, in chaos, in stress, in disease, and in imbalance. You can choose to stay balanced. You can choose to stay in peace. You can choose to see any such event or experience in your personal life or around the world as a gift, and you can choose to be a wayshower and to guide others to navigate that time with greater ease and grace.

No matter when you are reading this, know that there is more to come. There is always more to come. We do not say that to scare you or to overwhelm you. We say that to inspire you. You can choose to see experiences in your life and your world as devastation, or you can choose to see them as opportunities.

During such times, many people react to things they see or encounter—such as widespread fear of isolation or of lack and scarcity, watching economic markets and the news—and go into a state of panic or stress, which creates a response within the human body of fight or flight. That is a very basic humanistic response to stress and fear. You go into survival mode, fight or flight. When you do that, you significantly lower your level of consciousness, your level of intelligence, and your level of awareness, which moves you into an environment, a state of consciousness, and an experience where you feel helpless, victimized, and out of control. You are trying to grasp at any ability to control, and you will find yourself having a very chaotic experience.

There is a level of consciousness and awareness available to you, and you can choose at any time to elevate yourself out of fight-or-flight mode into alignment, awareness, and a state of fully opening and allowing energy to guide you. Energy will always guide the way for you if you will allow it, but energy and light cannot guide you if you are in fight-or-flight mode.

You can choose at any time to elevate yourself into alignment, awareness, and a state of fully opening and allowing energy to guide you. Energy will always guide the way for you if you will allow it.

When there is mass conscious hysteria and fear in the media, it can cause you to move into a dimension of consciousness where you are not rationally evaluating and choosing within your experience. We understand that these situations and events are very real on your planet as they occur. We do not disagree. We also understand that there is often hype around them or a fear associated with them that contributes to creating a frenzy. The frenzy then readily allows a perspective or a way of perceiving information that creates a great amount of unconsciousness, reaction, and resistance. When you take in information from fight-or-flight mode, that state does not allow you to navigate the information rationally and reasonably in a way that you do not go into fear.

Many of you have come to a level of consciousness and awareness where, when you're really in the *knowing*, you are not afraid of death. Yet the frenzy and the media attention around a particular event can still create a sudden fear where all at once you are afraid of your own death, and if you're not afraid of your own death then you're afraid of your parents' deaths or your friends' deaths. Then you can find yourself in hysterical fear of death or of how you're going to die or of suffering.

We remind you, because it's really important, that the experience you call death is merely a transition. In one breath someone transitions out of the density of the human body and into pure blissful, all-knowing love. If one is choosing to make their transition through some particular event, you must remember that you will cause your own suffering if you think you know what another soul's journey should be. You do not. You do not, just like with any other transition, just like in any other experience. There are many people who contract with particular events or circumstances to make their transitions when their experiences here in human form are complete. *Honor that.* Don't try to go into a frenzy and control it or prevent it.

You have the ability to stay conscious and present. You have the wisdom, you have the information, you have the knowledge, you have the skills, and you have the tools to rise above the fear and the chaos and to be wayshowers of a better way during events or situations that may be considered challenging. Those are the times that *you matter,* your choices matter, your consciousness matters, and your ability to stay present and in your heart and allow energy to guide you matters. It matters now, and it matters more than ever during times of great change. Those are the times that you can really live everything you know.

We say this with such great love. Do not entangle with the suffering, with the chaos, with the trauma, with the fear, with the frenzy. If you are feeling any of those things, you are choosing to go down into the fear and the density instead of staying in your truth, in your knowing, and in your power, and there's no judgment from our side ever.

We remind you that you are the wayshowers, that you are *here* to help bring about great change. You are *here* to help guide your beloved human family through the greatest awakening of human consciousness that has ever occurred on your planet. You *cannot* do that if you are in fear. You *cannot* do that if you yourself are in a state of chaos. You do it by consciously rising above whatever may be happening to a state of awareness where the fear and the chaos do not exist and therefore the specifics of the situation are not significant.

You are here to help guide your human family through the greatest awakening that has ever occurred on your planet.

There are often questions about particular entities, circumstances, and events as they arise or come into your awareness. We'll begin by telling you that everything is infinite intelligence, no different than you, no different than the animal kingdom, no different than the plant kingdom, no different than the star systems—no different. Everything is part of the existence of the Divine. It is part of something greater. It has a purpose, just like you. Whatever it may be, it has a purpose for being part of the current experience, just like everything else on this planet at this time. It has a purpose. You cause your own suffering when you *think* you know what another's purpose is, what another soul's purpose is, what another system of existence is here to do.

We invite you into a radical way of thinking about these things, although somewhere inside of you it will feel more like truth than a radical truth. Whatever you may be thinking of, encountering, or experiencing, it has an intelligence. It has a purpose for being here. It is of the Divine. It is of infinite intelligence. It is of God.

In many cases, there is an available awareness upfront that statistically, measurably, based on numbers and mathematics, the situation is not as out of control, deadly, horrific, or terrible as your media may make it out to be. There are reasons why that occurs, and we *do not* contribute to beliefs in conspiracy. If you believe that to be your truth, so it is. However, we would say that the reason for the media's representation of things is that they are reflecting where most people's consciousness and thinking and power lie, which is in giving control to someone outside of them, giving control to everything outside of them, feeling helpless and powerless.

When you turn up the knob a little bit, as we said, things are going to get accelerated. Things are going through a quickening. You are going to see a quickening occurring, and when you accelerate anything, you will get more of what is really there. If it's fear, fear will come to the surface faster. The chaos will come to the surface faster, the love will come to the surface faster, or the peace will come to the surface faster—whatever is really there. Anytime you have a media frenzy, you tend to look at it, and if you are in fear or if you are in fight or flight, you will not choose the conscious view. You will not stay open. You will not see the grander perspective or the higher viewpoint. We remind you to be aware that the numbers and the mathematics are often not equal to the level of frenzy and chaos that is being experienced.

We also remind you that everything, everything, *if you choose to see it this way*, is the existence of the Divine, is the existence of God, is the existence of some grander plan. Will you deny the existence of God within you and your ability to navigate a situation or event? Will you deny the existence of God in others and their ability to navigate an experience? Will you deny the existence of God in the situation and decide that it's terrible and awful and things are out of control, or will you stay in the knowing, in the greater awareness of what's *really* going on?

As we said, it is the feeling of being out of control that causes a great amount of your discomfort and discord, the feeling of losing your freedom to do what you want to do when you want to do it or your freedom to be who you are. We assure you there is *absolutely no possible way whatsoever* that an event or a set of circumstances or a government can take your freedom or your ability to maintain a level of openness and allowing such that you always have everything you need and more. Your government could even decide that you cannot move about your community or your town, and you could feel out of control and stuck or unfree to do what you wish to do. Yet in that situation, most of you would feel a lack of freedom more so because of the thoughts that you are thinking than because of anything your government had imposed on you. You only find freedom through your thinking.

Your thoughts, your feelings, your state of consciousness are the only places where you will find freedom. When your mind and your consciousness and your awareness find freedom, your body will feel free, balanced, and at ease.

———

You only find freedom through your thinking and your state of consciousness. When your mind and your consciousness and your awareness find freedom, your body will feel free, balanced, and at ease.

———

There is frequently a great amount of focus on control, on controlling things, on controlling circumstances, on controlling people, and that usually leads to the feeling of being out of control or of not having control. We want to remind you that this is not so. *You absolutely have a choice.* You can choose to entangle with any situation, and you can choose to rise above it. You can choose to be at peace. You can choose to see whatever happens as a gift and an opportunity. The truth is, that is the only way. Really.

Here's the best part. We have told you time and time again that *one* of you fully opening and allowing the power of the Source to flow through you, *one* of you in an elevated state of consciousness, allowing the highest vibration of the truth of who you are, *one* of you fully standing in your power with an open heart, in a state of peace and love and freedom and harmony, is more powerful than millions who are not. No matter what may or may not be happening around you, this is the time—more than ever before—for you to stand in your power, shine your light, be all that you are, and maintain the highest level of consciousness, which means maintaining *absolute balance* within you and around you. If there is balance within you, there will be balance around you.

There are countless reasons for your feeling the way you do in a situation. Perhaps your friends or family are afraid or even freaking out about an event. You may feel vulnerable or susceptible, or you may be concerned that someone you care about is at risk. However, if you are choosing to entangle with the fear, then in that moment you are adding to the fear. As we have said, those feelings of unconsciousness will be more awful than ever before because you have been in the truth, you have been at the highest levels of consciousness and awareness, and you know who you are. Be all that you are. Be the wayshowers of a better way. Take a breath and get into a place of peace within you. Peace does not come from *out there*. It comes from within you. It's an alignment to the peace that is within you.

Regardless of circumstances or appearances, there is no need for you to buy into frenzy or fear. You do not have to entangle with anything. In any experience that you or others might consider challenging, the most important thing that you can do is, first and foremost, remember the process of creating what you want *more* of within you and in the field around you. If others are in fear, don't perpetuate the fear. Don't go down into fear. Don't contribute to chaos. Stop, take a breath, come back to a conscious place in the here and now, and ask yourself, *What is it that I want? I want peace for them. I want balance. I want harmony. I want ease—* whatever it is. *I want freedom.* Then go into your heart, find the peace that is within you, and align to that peace.

If you really want to do something to help your human family during such an experience or at any time—because one of you who is connected to the truth and the power within you is more powerful than millions who are not—then go within you and find the peace that lies within you. Turn it on, activate it, ignite it. Align every single cell of your body to the state of peace, to the state of freedom, to the state of harmony, to the state of well-being, and see that infused in the light of your being. In the light of your being infuse peace, infuse harmony, infuse balance, infuse freedom. Send it out to the heart of every single person you know and love, every single person you will ever know and love, and every single person that they know and love. Sit in your power and see the love and the peace and the harmony and the balance going from your heart through your light to the hearts of everyone, and know that they can remember and awaken to the truth within them to also live in peace and joy and harmony, no matter what is going on *out there.*

The world around you is a reflection of the world that exists within you. The answer in any situation or experience is consciousness and love and choosing the highest perspective, the highest outcome. It is your perspective that will determine whether you experience the highest outcome, the highest good, the highest potential of any and every situation. You can *absolutely choose* to see it as happening *for* you, happening *for* humanity, happening *for* the planet. And so it is, because it *is*. No matter what it is, it is bringing balance. It is bringing restoration. It is bringing transformation. It is bringing consciousness.

Your perspective determines whether you experience the highest outcome, the highest potential of any and every situation.

You have been *asking* for balance with the environment. You have been *asking* for balance within your human family, and you've been *asking* for balance within your own being. That's what the events in your world are bringing. You have been asking for consciousness. You've been asking for transformation, and you have been asking, because you know it's why you're here, to see the Great Awakening happen right before your eyes, and so it is. If you will stay conscious in your awareness through it all, you will always see the *absolute love*, the absolute potential here, the absolute highest perspective. Circumstances and events are ushering in the change. They are ushering in the Great Awakening. They are ushering in a more beautiful future. They are ushering in a new paradigm. It's so important that you stay conscious.

They can also create a level of survival mode, a level of fight or flight where people do not think reasonably, where people do not think—we'll even say it—logically, intelligently, or consciously. In that case, many are willing to settle and accept things. They're willing to allow things because they're not staying conscious and they're not staying present and they're not staying at a level of balance or awareness. This can mean that they'll allow things that they would never have otherwise allowed by those around them, by political parties, by governments, by a hierarchical power.

It is *extremely* important that you stay conscious, no matter the circumstances. It is *extremely* important that you stay in your heart, in your consciousness, in your well-being, and in an internal state of peace and harmony. It is really important. It's *really* important that you step into being the master that you are and not a fearful human who is in fight or flight, panic, chaos, reaction, suffering, or trauma. It's really important, especially because your choosing to be in your power throughout these situations allows the potential for you to bring peace and joy and harmony and seed human consciousness in times when it is needed most. That is why you're here. That is why you're here. *That is why you're here.*

The next 10 years are going to be a global awakening for millions of people, an awakening to who they are, to what's really going on here, to their connection to the Source, to their connection to one another and to the planet, to energy, to all of the different ecosystems that support them, and to come into balance with them all.

We don't say any of that from some level of judging anything *at all* as wrong or bad or devastating or terrible. When you want to say things like that or you hear things like that or the media reports things like that, we invite you to become aware and to not buy into and contribute to and entangle with the fearful, unconscious survival response. We want to say with such great love—and we really mean it—you know better. *You know better.* You know better because you know who you are. You know the truth within you of who you are and why you're here, of how important you are to seeding human consciousness with a higher perspective and a grander possibility of a more harmonious, peaceful, abundant, loving, beautiful world.

The circumstances do not ever change your ability in any way to choose to live in Heaven on Earth *right here, right now, and in every moment.* There is magic here for you. There are miracles here for you. There is incredible momentum here for you. There are opportunities here for you. There are gifts here for you. There are blessings here for you. There is love here for you. There is guidance here for you. There is light here for you. It's all here for you. Everything you could ever need and more is here for you now.

Every single one of you would tell us that you want to serve, that you want to help people, that you want to make a difference, that you want to create a better world, that you want to see positive change. Yet when you have the opportunity, you often go into fear, suffering, chaos, reaction, survival mode, and fight or flight. Yet you want to help people. *You can,* and these experiences are your opportunities. They are your times to make a difference. You can do so individually and collectively. We are also here because we promised we would be, to guide you through such things. We are here to stay in the light so that you never forget the way, so that you never forget who you are, so that you never forget how important you are. Now more than ever, stay in peace. Stay in your heart. Stay open and allow. Find the peace within. Find the harmony within. Be the peace. Be the light. Be the harmony. Be the better way. Be the wayshowers. Be all that you are.

If you want to make a difference like never before, then be rare and unique. Be one who is walking around during what most perceive as challenging times with joy in your heart, a sparkle in your eye, and a smile on your face, being uplifting, being lighthearted, being joyful, being hopeful, being happy, being loving, being kind. If you want to attract abundance and light and love and joy and connection like never before, be all that you are *now more than ever.* Be the master that you are. Be in your power. Hold your head up high. Put a smile on your face. Let the light twinkle in your eye. Let the love of your heart radiate for all to see. You have any and every opportunity to connect more so than ever, here and now, even if the circumstances happen to appear otherwise.

Whenever you are reading this is truly an incredible time. Living a magical life is about *redefining* potentials and possibilities and your ability to create the world you want to live in. It is more important now than ever that you hold the vision of a New Earth, of Heaven on Earth, of all beings who choose to live in Heaven on Earth experiencing peace, joy, love, abundance, harmony with each other, with the animals, with the land, even with the viruses, the bacteria, the ecosystems, and all things that are of the Source. All things are of the Divine and have an intelligence and a purpose for being here.

———

Living a magical life is about redefining
potentials and possibilities and your ability
to create the world you want to live in.
Hold the vision of Heaven on Earth.

———

If you embrace it, bless it, and send it love, any event, situation, or thing can complete its purpose in an expeditious fashion and return to the light where all beings and extensions of the Source will inevitably return. Hear this with great importance. Whatever the circumstance may be, bless it, thank it for coming, send it love, and it will return to the light *expeditiously,* and with seemingly no explanation other than this one: those who are in their power are more powerful than the millions who are not in their power.

You will see the situation complete its purpose of bringing balance and restoration and transformation and awakening, and you will witness it return to the light in the most expeditious fashion. Support it in its purpose, bless it in its purpose, love it for a job well done, and it will return to the light with little-to-no explanation. But you will know. You will know the power that you have, the power of love, the power of consciousness, the power of collective consciousness, the power of each and every one of you holding the highest state of consciousness in a state of pure love.

Bless it, thank it, love it, and it will return to the light. And if ever again it comes back into your experience or the human experience, you will remember and you will know that it is only here because it has a purpose to serve, just like you. You are here because you have a purpose to serve. This is your purpose. *Live it, love it, and be all that you are.* There is nothing to fear. There is no need to pretend you are powerless, no need. There is no need to hold yourself in a lower dimension of consciousness. There is no need to suffer. Anything that you experience is just an opportunity for you to remember.

Whenever you see a slowing down of life's day-to-day responsibilities or tasks, know that is also for you. During those times there's something emerging through each and every one of you in the way of your *gifts*, in the way of your *abilities*, in the way of your *talents*, in the way of your *wisdom*. Things happen to offer you the opportunity, the time, and the space to allow it in. It's only then that you can allow it in fully and expeditiously, because you have the time and space to focus on *you* and your gifts and your connection to the Source, on the awareness and the wisdom that's coming through you, and on your abilities and your talents— none of which you learned in this human experience, but you are remembering them now.

See the slowing down as space and time that you are *gifted*, that you are granted, and receive it. Let it be joyful. Let it be *fun*. Have fun with it. That does not mean you stop playing, and it *certainly* doesn't mean you stop creating. You are creating every moment, whether you know it or not. You're either creating more fear or chaos, or you're creating peace and a better world and a New Earth and the opportunity for humanity, if they so choose, to elevate their consciousness and therefore their experience to a state of pure love, pure light, oneness, total harmony, total balance, and total freedom. And so it is.

We bring this message to you with great love for you. We bring this message to you with great respect for you. We bring this message to you with our sincerest gratitude for your courage, for stepping into the human experience, for being the wayshowers that you are, for bringing about the greatest change and the Great Awakening of humanity at an unprecedented rate unseen before. We assure you, while the potential and the possibility for Heaven on Earth exists for all of humanity, it is more important than ever that you choose it for *yourself now*. And so it is.

———

**The possibility for Heaven on Earth
exists for all of humanity, and it is important
that you choose it for yourself now.**

———

ESSENTIAL MESSAGES

- Whatever you are feeling in the moment is what you are contributing to human consciousness.

- You are the wayshowers here to help guide your beloved human family through the greatest awakening of human consciousness that has ever occurred on your planet.

- Your state of consciousness is the only place where you will find freedom.

- The potential for you to be in your power is the potential for you to bring peace and joy and harmony and seed human consciousness in a time when it is needed most.

- Living a magical life is about *redefining* potentials and possibilities and your ability to create the world you want to live in.

- You can choose at any time to elevate yourself into alignment, awareness, and fully opening and allowing energy to guide you. Energy will always guide the way for you if you will allow it.

- The possibility for Heaven on Earth exists for all of humanity, and it is important that you choose it for yourself now.

CHAPTER TEN

THE POTENTIAL FOR A FULLY AWAKENED WORLD

In this chapter, The Council offers insight into the opportunity available to take a quantum leap into a new experience and the potential to live in a fully awakened world.

We are so pleased and delighted to have the opportunity to speak with you on this fine day indeed. We know that there are often events around your world that make it appear as if there are certain challenging times in your human experience. We know that it sometimes appears as if major change is underway. And we assure you *it is*. Whatever may be happening in your world, we are here to remind you of what you never intended to forget when you chose this magnificent life experience.

There are many, many beings in a higher level of consciousness who are aware of you, guiding you, and here for you always. You are *never* alone, we assure you. Even in the moments when you feel the most fear, the most vulnerable, and the most alone, we assure you that you could not be. There are so many here focused on you with love, focusing a higher awareness and a higher conscious-ness, holding a higher awareness, holding a higher consciousness so that, in your moments of allowing, you can reconnect with the truth within you and remember who you are and why you are here during this time of the Great Awakening of your human family.

When there is global change underway, many of you experience a great amount of emotion, and we want to remind you why. You experience a great amount of emotion because you so deeply love your human family. Many of you often go through the motions of life and find yourselves frequently triggered and in reaction to your human family. In fact, you do that more than you remember the love that you have for humanity. If you did not have such love for humanity, you would not be here.

You came forth into this life experience, and your *entire* life experience has been preparing you for this Great Awakening. However, more specifically, the past 10 years of your human experience have been preparing you for this time. Many of you have seen a quickening and an acceleration during the past few years. You have noticed that there seems to have been a sense of urgency to remember, to gain a higher level of consciousness, to elevate your vibration, and to create an experience of Heaven on Earth within your own life. All of that has been preparing you for this time now.

Your human family is going through the Great Awakening. It has moved into an accelerated phase where millions of people are going to awaken, just as you have, to the truth within them.

Awakening is a journey. It is a journey that you *never* complete so long as you're in the human experience. There is always more. There are always elevated levels of consciousness. There is always an opportunity to accelerate your knowing and to raise your vibration to allow more energy, more light, and more awareness into the human experience, into your human experience.

The times of quickening and acceleration help prepare you for global events. We remind you, *everything has a purpose and reason for being on the planet*, just like you have a purpose for being on this planet. We tell you with a sense of urgency and importance to acknowledge, accept, and choose to align with the truth of your experience, which is that this is the most important time for the awakening of your human family and the opportunity for a raising of consciousness like never before.

Do not be in a hurry to eliminate any discomfort that you may feel. Do not be in a hurry to complete an event or experience. Do not be in a hurry to rid the world of some circumstance or situation. Allow it all to serve its purpose. If you remember how to get into a state of peace and align to the peace that lies within you, how to find an inner balance and an inner harmony, you will navigate each and every experience in your life with great ease and without any resistance about how long anything lasts.

—

If you remember how to get to a state of peace and inner harmony, you will navigate your life experiences with great ease.

—

Many people went through their own personal awakening experiences over many years' time. Some went through their awakening experiences in a very short amount of time. Either way, for most people, awakening has come in times of discomfort where things *had* to change. However, they were resisting the change because of fear, because of not remembering their power, because they didn't remember that there was a greater purpose for their lives, because they didn't understand that there was a grander perspective of what was going on in life than what they could see or remember. The same is true in the Great Awakening.

Whether a particular event, circumstance, or occurrence lasts a few weeks or several months is based on the free-will choices of many, many, many people who chose that time and that experience for their awakening. Keep in mind that such events, global or otherwise, happen *for* you. These experiences happen for you to step into higher dimensions of consciousness and seed human consciousness with a grander perspective to create a new paradigm of human existence and create paradigms within the human experience that are of a higher vibration and a higher consciousness, which will bring greater love, greater joy, greater peace, greater harmony, and greater cooperation to all of humanity, to the planet, and to animal life.

You are going to continue experiencing innovation at a level that is unprecedented. You have seen a speeding up of technological innovation for the past many years, but this phase of the Great Awakening is going to bring about innovation at a level you've never seen before in all sorts of categories.

Allow it. Allow events and experiences to take however long they need. Allow them to take whatever time is appropriate for *something really important* to happen in human consciousness. If you are in resistance and pushing against, you are not holding the space to *allow* the grander perspective to unfold and the Great Awakening to occur. It can absolutely happen with ease and grace for all, but that is not always the way it happens because so many are in resistance and in fear and experiencing chaos. Remember that in every moment, whatever you are feeling within you is what you are contributing to humanity or to the greater whole at that moment.

You have incredible opportunities to start creating and living in new paradigms of consciousness within the human experience. It starts with *you* creating a new paradigm within *you*. This very moment is a gift and an opportunity to look at your life, your choices, your thinking, your behavior, your health, your well-being, your relationships, your purpose, your passion, your joys, and to transform your life to be everything you wish it to be *here and now.*

———

**This moment is a gift and an opportunity
to transform your life to be everything you
wish it to be here and now.**

———

As you make the transformations within you and create a new paradigm within you, you then begin to create a new paradigm within your families, within your communities, and within the world as a whole. But it starts with you, and then it extends into your direct proximity. From there it extends into your family circles and friend circles, and then it extends into your communities.

The opportunity to create a new paradigm within human existence is available to you now. You have the time, the space, and the freedom right here and now to hold the vision of a New Earth moving into form within the human experience. With a whole lot of love, you will see transformation occur like never before. As time passes, many people will align and begin to find what they need within them and around them. You will make the most of the technology that you have, and you will make the most of the consciousness and awareness available to create great innovation within your own lives.

That great innovation will offer you a *different* experience as you move forward. You are being offered an opportunity, truly, to take a quantum leap into a whole new experience. Pause and consider how reliant you have been on just doing what you thought you should do or what you have always done instead of consciously questioning whether it was aligned or if that is where energy was leading you or guiding you to go.

———

You are being offered an opportunity to take a quantum leap into a whole new experience.

———

For instance, at some point you may have thought, *Well, I miss my loved one, so I need to jump on an airplane and go see them.* Yet that often created *greater* separation from the people you love in your life because you limited the experience of being together to mean only *geographically* being together. Instead of having a deep connection with them, you usually waited for that connection to occur when you could be together in person. However, during times when you believed that option was not available for whatever reason, you were more likely to choose to reach out in the *now* and connect, and to love and to communicate with those who matter most to you in any and every way that was possible for you.

You are using the technology that's in place for connection. You are using the technology that is in place for information. You are using the technology that is in place for innovation, and you're going to see that you just get *more*. As another example, there were times in the past when you were accustomed to going somewhere anytime you wanted to connect with others. Whether you were used to going somewhere for a particular activity or used to going somewhere for entertainment, you have since found the means of bringing all of those things to you through innovation. You're going to continue to find that you can be far more efficient, and have a much greater experience of space and time in your life where you can flow and allow energy to serve and guide you.

Whenever you are reading this is truly a magical time if you will allow it to be. As you focus on creating your own Heaven on Earth, it may almost feel constricting in certain ways, although it's not. In fact, it's quite the contrary. Allow your focus to be on creating your own Heaven on Earth here and now and then on holding the vision for a grander perspective to emerge as you create new paradigms of human existence. In some cases, these tremendous paradigm shifts can *only* come from experiences of extraordinary transformation occurring at one time globally.

We are going to say something very important to you, and we want you to understand this: Remember that each and every one of you is here in this experience for your *own* expansion, your *own* experience, your *own* expression of all that you are. If you're reading this, you're here as part of the Great Awakening, but you are also here to create your *own* Heaven on Earth and experience it to the *fullest*.

You have the *real* potential to live in a fully awakened world by the year 2035 in Earth time, where all beings that remain on the planet are living in a higher dimension of consciousness, fully awakened and aware of the truth *within* them. This does not mean that all will experience their awakening through the spiritual path that many of you have taken. Still, it is a raising of the consciousness on the planet where people will live at a higher rate of vibration and frequency and therefore experience the level of peace and joy and harmony that exists within those higher dimensions of consciousness. You will live in a world where *all* beings live harmoniously with each other, with the animals, with the land, and with the planet, and, most importantly, all beings will live harmoniously within *themselves*.

**You will live in a world where all beings
live harmoniously with each other and
within themselves.**

This is important, and there's a reason for it. There's a reason that the Great Awakening is important. There's a reason it's happening at this time. It is still a *potential* because there are a great amount of free-will choices that each and every one of you has. However, as we have said, you can live in a fully awakened world by 2035, but many, many more need to be awakened over the next few years for this to occur. That is why you have seen so many global events recently. That is why your life prepared you for such experiences.

There is an intelligence here. It does not mitigate your free-will choices, and it also doesn't mean that you are here to serve and sacrifice and suffer to drag your entire human family over the finish line into an awakened state. That is not what we are saying.

We are saying that the most important thing that you can do is create the Heaven on Earth that is available to you and live fully conscious and awakened and aware within your own creation of reality. In that reality, most of you are going to choose to create new paradigms within human existence that are based on a higher perspective, a higher state of consciousness. From a more awakened and aware viewpoint, you are so conscious of your *every* action and choice, of how it affects you and how it affects the world around you. You are so conscious of your ability to create the reality you live in and your *assured* potential to transcend fear and suffering and chaos and tragedy and lack, not only in your human experience, but in the entire human experience.

That is what the Great Awakening presents you with: the potential as a human family to *collectively* elevate your consciousness out of fear and lack and suffering forevermore to an experience of joy, peace, harmony, and abundance for all. It is not your job to figure out how to do all of that. It's your job to hold the vision and create it for *yourself,* to live it now, to choose it now, to be it now, and to allow it to express fully through you.

—

**The Great Awakening presents you with the potential
to collectively elevate your consciousness out of fear
and lack into harmony and abundance.**

—

There's much more to come, and we have much more for you. We do not see any time as tragic. We know if you turn on the news and you see some trauma or drama or suffering, it is hard to understand how that could ever be happening for some greater purpose. When you come into the human experience, you often learn to fear making your transition out of the human experience more than anything else, and so much emphasis is placed on the fear of death, the fear of how you're going to die, the fear of suffering your way to death. It does not have to be that way for *anyone*, but we understand that it's still what many experience. During times of what many may call great tragedy, see that those who are making their transitions are surrounded in *light*, surrounded in *peace*.

When you want something for others, when you see others in fear or chaos or suffering, it is so important that you decide in that moment, as the conscious Creator that you are, what it is that *you* choose. What do *you* want more of in that moment? What do you want for *you*, and what do you want for *them*? You don't get to choose for them, but you do get to choose for you. By choosing something greater for you, it helps others to remember that a grander potential and possibility is available for them just as it is for you. It makes it easier for them to find their way back to the peace within them that is always available to them as well.

When you see others suffering, ask yourself what *you* want at that moment. Come into the present moment and take a breath. *What do I want here? What do I want more of? What do I want to create?* If the answer is peace, then go into *your own being* and feel the peace that is within you and activate *every* cell of your body to align with that peace. Then focus that feeling of peace so strongly that it is radiating from your being in every direction all around you and see it going out into the hearts of all of those that you love and care about and wish peace for. This is something you can always do.

——

**Come into the present moment and ask yourself:
What do I want more of? What do I want to create?**

——

When you say, *well, there's suffering going on in the world*, and you turn on the television and see the suffering that's happening *out there*, we want to remind you that it is not happening in your direct energy field unless, through your focus and attention, you draw it to you. When you look at others' experiences *out there*, because your televisions give you some perspective, you are often actually suffering worse than the people who are in the experience. You truly are. We're not saying that they're not suffering, but we're saying that you do not have to choose to suffer yourself. In that moment that they really are in that experience, they have an energy, an awareness, a Source that is guiding them because they're *in* that experience. You cannot observe it from a television perspective without creating a great amount of suffering for yourself, even though your direct experience in *your* world has the potential to be a peaceful, joyful, heavenly one.

If you *are* one who is personally impacted by a particular event or situation or you *are* interacting with those affected by such an experience in your daily life or vocation, we tell you that you are so incredibly guided, supported, loved, and held in the light by all those in higher dimensions of consciousness and greater frequencies of light in *every* moment, and if you will open to that, you will *feel* it. You will feel a sense of peace, a sense of well-being.

Remember, you always have a choice. You always have a light that is guiding you. In every moment you can always elevate your consciousness and therefore elevate your experience out of fear and chaos and trauma and suffering. This is the truth, and somewhere within you know it, or you wouldn't be reading this now.

We are here to remind you of the truth within you. We are here because we promised we would be, especially now. You drew this information to you because it belongs to you. It's the truth within you that you never intended to forget—the truth of who you are, why you are here, and the power that you have to create in this human experience and to hold the highest perspective of a better way and a new paradigm that is emerging. You are here to illuminate the potential for humankind.

Remember who you are. Remember why you are here. Remember how important you are. If there is a time when you may *feel* like you are not free to be the wayshower that you are, to connect the way you wish to, or to do the things you wish to do, maybe it's because there's something better trying to present itself to you. Maybe there's something better than the things you thought were so important every day. Maybe there's something more. Maybe there's something more awakening within you. Maybe there's something even better than how you were living your life, and that very experience has been orchestrated for you to allow something bigger, something greater, to express itself through you or to present itself to you.

Maybe there's something even better than how you were living your life, and this very experience has been orchestrated for you to allow something greater to present itself to you.

We are always with you. We are always available to you. This is a time when many of you are going to awaken to gifts and talents and abilities that you know you have somewhere within you, even if you don't really know what they are. Many of you know there's some greater purpose for your life. Many of you know there's some greater calling, some greater purpose, some greater knowing that you have, but for whatever reason your day-to-day life distractions didn't allow you to tune in to fully remember until now.

Let all things unfold with ease and grace. Let it all come in its time and in its way. Our only ask of you is to stay open and allow and let energy light the way. What better time to become an *absolute master* at allowing energy to guide the way than this time now? In this awareness, you now have a greater potential to follow the energy and the light and what you're guided to each day instead of all the things you used to think you *had* to do.

This experience is a gift; you are also a gift to humanity and to those around you and those you love. Be all that you are. Live all that you know. Be the wayshower that you are of a better way forward. You are the Creator within your own creation. You *are* creating every moment. Right now, you have the greatest opportunity to completely transcend the unwanted, the limitation, the old story, and to create your entire experience anew in a new world, in a new paradigm, where *anything* and *everything* is possible for you.

Let this very day be a sacred time for you to take a moment and connect to the *highest vision possible* for your life experience. Then create it starting now and *live it* in this moment here and now and forevermore.

There is a purpose for everything that happens. There is a purpose for you. You always have the ability to choose—in every moment—what you are contributing and what you are creating. There is a potential here for the most incredible transformation of human consciousness that has ever occurred in any lifetime. There is the potential for innovation that will greatly expand your role in the universe. There's a reason for humanity to awaken, because on the other side of an awakened human family is a grander potential for Earth and humanity in the vast and beautiful universe.

We remind you that you are everything you wish to be. You already are, and we love you, we love you, *we love you*. And so it is.

——

You are everything you wish to be. You already are.

——

ESSENTIAL MESSAGES

- This is the most important time for the awakening of your human family and an opportunity for a raising of consciousness like never before.

- You have the time, the space, the freedom right here and now to hold the vision of a New Earth moving into form within the human experience.

- The most important thing that you can do is create the Heaven on Earth that is available to you and live fully conscious and awakened and aware within your own creation of reality.

- You can elevate your consciousness and therefore elevate your experience out of fear and chaos and trauma and suffering.

- You have the greatest opportunity to completely transcend the unwanted, the limitation, the old story, and to create your entire experience anew in a new world, in a new paradigm, where *anything* and *everything* is possible for you.

- If you remember how to get to a state of peace and inner harmony, you will navigate your life experiences with great ease.

CHAPTER ELEVEN

IMPECCABLE CREATION OF A RICHER, FULLER EXPERIENCE

In this chapter, The Council reminds you of the power of impeccable creative expression and following the energy because everything is a result of your creation.

We are so pleased and delighted to have the opportunity to speak with you, our beloved friend. We are here for you at this time where you are stepping into being the fully realized master of your life experience that you are. We are speaking to *you*. We are speaking to *you*. It is here, and it is now. It is the time for you to be all that you are, to live in your Heaven on Earth, and to be part of this Great Awakening experience that you have been preparing for all of your life. We remind you that you have the power within you to do anything, to be anything, to have anything, and to draw anything and everything that is in your highest and best good to you, and *that applies here and now, no matter the circumstances*.

Have you noticed the manifestation of many of the things you've been asking for and wondered if that would ever happen in your life experience? Are you seeing people whom you love and care about starting to ask the question that you asked, the one that started you on this awakening journey in the first place? Do you know what question you asked that opened the doors to you? Do you remember the first time you asked the question that drew the experience of awakening to you?

It wasn't *How much money do I have?* It wasn't *Where is my lover?* It wasn't *How do I fix this broken body?* It wasn't *Why did they die?* It wasn't *What has gone wrong here?* The question you asked that started this entire awakening experience for you was *who am I? Who am I? Who am I?*

That is the question you asked. That is what started you on this journey. Life was not happening to you. It was happening for you to draw to you the experience that would answer that question for you. *Who am I?* That is what opens the door to your awakening journey.

Many are finding themselves in moments where the distractions are gone, where the rushing and the bustling through the day is no longer, and they are asking themselves the question, *who am I?* It may be some fear that leads them to ask that question. It may be a belief in lack that leads them to ask that question. It may be a misunderstanding of God or feeling like God has somehow allowed a particular situation or event to happen. But they are asking, *who am I?* And just like you, they also have a Source that is aware of them and available to them. They also have guides. They also have a higher self. They have all the things that you had and have that will draw to them the experiences that will guide them to a higher knowing and a higher truth and a higher perspective and a much grander experience and to know the answer to *who am I?*

Do you know the answer now? Because when you're ready to move from the awakening journey to the journey of the master, you know. The master knows *who I am.* The master knows I Am That I Am. The master knows I Am Creator. The master knows that I Am Presence. The master knows the mighty I Am Presence that you are. How could that *not* draw to you a more expansive, richer, more fulfilling, more harmonious, more beautiful, more exciting, more inspiring, more abundant experience of life and living it to the fullest? It will indeed.

We couldn't *be* more excited for you. You know who you are, and once you know the I Am Presence, you begin to play and dance and create with All That Is. You begin dancing with all of creation as the master that you are, practicing and mastering your ability to follow the energy and follow the light. It will always guide the way for you. You begin mastering impeccable, innocent, inspired creative expression that is dedicated to the highest good of *all* of humanity and the planet and all that exists.

We have told you that on the other side of a fully awakened human family there is so much more. There's so much more. There is a purpose for humanity in the vast, glorious, beautiful universe of limitless potential and possibility.

The master of one's life is no longer trying to create from lack or limitation or unworthiness. The master has no personal agenda. Most of you would say that you want to get to the place where you have no personal agenda, but it is merely a choice to align with the infinite abundance, the infinite well-being, the infinite love, the infinite connection to All That Is, and the infinite intelligence. That power is available to you at every moment and guides you always. It will provide everything you need and more, everything you could even imagine to ask for if you will allow it. Open and allow the energy to serve you and to serve through you as you follow the light and bring the powerful beacon of light that you are to the world around you. That is how important you are.

But the master creates impeccably from a place of innocence and inspiration with no personal agenda. They're not trying to *fix* anything. They're not trying to *heal* anything. They're not trying to *attract* a lover. They're not trying to make people do what they want them to do. They're not trying to make more money with the energy. It's impeccable. It's innocent. It's pure. It's inspired. And, oh, you can't even imagine the power you have when you *allow* the energy to flow through you without a personal agenda.

**Open and allow the power of true creation to flow
through you without a personal agenda.**

―

Having a personal agenda means that you try to *push* energy.
A personal agenda is present any time you're trying to *own* energy.
Your personal agenda shows up through your trying to *control*
energy. You have a personal agenda whenever you are in *lack* and
you think that if you had just that thing, you would no longer be
in lack—but that's not it at all.

In approaching creation this way, you are trying to draw
someone to you who will fulfill you and make you happy, or you
are trying to fix the part of you that you think is broken instead
of getting into a higher dimension of consciousness through your
vibration, by opening and allowing energy to serve you, where all
that you want is assured—your well-being, infinite love, infinite
abundance. From that state of consciousness, you don't *need* to go
down into the limitation, the lack, the suffering, the struggle, the
forcing, the efforting in order to create more because nothing is
wrong or missing.

When you have a personal agenda, you're limiting energy.
You're limiting creation. You are dipping down into lower dimensions of consciousness that you've already ascended beyond. You
are playing at greater levels of limitation, which is going to feel
like a struggle. That experience isn't going to feel very good and is
not going to be very uplifting.

This is why we tell you how important it is to transcend fear,
to transcend suffering, to transcend lack, to transcend worry and
pain. Most importantly, you can transcend fear and the belief in
your own limitation. You can transcend suffering in your own
human experience to open up the richest, most expansive level of
experience you could imagine.

You haven't even scratched the surface of how rich and abundant and prosperous your life is going to be when you get beyond

the personal agenda. Open up, allow energy to serve you, and practice *impeccable, innocent, inspired* creative expression that is dedicated to the highest outcome, the highest good of all, the highest and best. Then you do not limit the potential and the possibilities that are here for you.

――

You haven't even scratched the surface of how abundant your lives are going to be when you get beyond the personal agenda and practice impeccable, innocent, inspired creative expression.

――

Only you can decide. Only you can decide to stop rolling the boulder up the hill, in the mud, with the big heavy boots on and instead live on a mountaintop in Heaven on Earth. It's more important now than ever before that you do, really, truly. Whatever it is that keeps you from it, let it go. Let it go.

Sometimes it is about balancing your own system, and whenever you are reading this is a good time to focus on bringing your own system into balance. There are times where you have seen nature move back into total balance in the most *expeditious* and *efficient* ways. The oceans, the air, the forest, the trees, the birds, and the animals all start coming back into perfect, harmonious balance with each other without any assistance from humanity— that is, if humanity is not adding to the imbalance. You have seen your waters run cleaner during such times. You have seen your air cleaner and more pure. You have witnessed harmony in nature return at *expeditious* rates.

Nature *always* seeks to come into balance in the easiest, most effortless, expeditious way when you are not adding to and contributing to the imbalance. The rebalancing examples that humanity has witnessed during certain times are manifestations of what you ask for when you hold the vision of a New Earth, of Heaven on Earth, where all beings live in harmony with each other, with the animals, and with the planet, and within themselves. You have seen and will continue to see manifestations of it before your eyes.

There is a purpose for every event that transpires on your planet, and through those events people change. But it's not the chaos that changes them. It's not the fear that changes them. It is the love that changes them. If you want to continue to see the greatest opportunity for change in human consciousness, love them like never before. Love, love, love them like never before. Love your neighbor. Love your friends. Love your human family. Love the animals. Love the planet. Be the love that you are. You can't even imagine the divine love, the infinite love within your own being. You've never allowed yourself to really experience it in form. Allowing that would be to know yourself as the absolute God that you are. The almighty power that creates worlds is divine, infinite love. That is what your world needs most from you now, and always. Impeccable creative expression is always aligned with the infinite love of All That Is.

———

Be the love that you are. That is what your world needs most from you now, and always.

———

It is important that you find balance within your own life. What has to change in your own life? Don't push against it. Don't judge it. Don't go into resistance. Let it come from an inspired place. Let the change be bathed in love and purity and innocence.

For some, the change will be in your day-to-day behaviors and thinking and choices. For others it will be in finding clarity about what you want to experience more of in Heaven on Earth. For still others it will be reaching out and connecting in ways you haven't done before. And for some of you, it is an incredible change where, for the first time, you're allowing yourself to access certain talents, skills, and abilities that you have not yet experienced in human form. Most notably, you are able to access telepathic communication with others and with the highest information, opening your own channels to receive guidance and wisdom and inspiration and messages. You are allowing the healing light of the Source to flow through you like never before, opening up your creative fields to skills and abilities and talents that you've never known yourself to have.

This is an incredible time. Whenever you are reading this, it's an incredible time. So much is changing, and the change can be so much easier if you allow it with love. You're going to emerge from this part of your personal human experience truly living in a whole different world, in a much richer experience, a much more expanded experience, fully allowing infinite abundance, infinite love, and infinite well-being to be your reality.

Don't try to figure anything out right now. Don't make any big decisions. Don't try to change things in the way you used to do it. Don't try to force anything. In the doing, there's always more to be done. In the *being*, all things are done through you. It all comes to you. The path unfolds with ease and grace. It's choiceless. It's just clear, and you are totally confident. There is a certainty, and it just happens.

Don't try to figure anything out. *Don't* try to make any big decisions. There's no big decision. There's *no* big decision. There are no big decisions you need to make. There is only the simple decision of choosing to open and allow energy, to be all that you are, to live in Heaven on Earth here and now. That's the choice, and it is available to you. Your thinking, your vibration, your state of consciousness, those are the choices you make. If you should move—not a decision to make right now. If you should leave this relationship—not a decision to make right now. If you should start a new relationship—not a decision to make right now. If you do all of these things and push and force and try to make something happen, you are limiting the energy that is trying to present itself to you in a new way and move you into a new expanded experience of all that is that you've *never* allowed yourself before. The energy is offering you a richer, fuller, more expansive experience of what it's like to live beyond limitation.

**Make the simple decision to open and allow
energy, to be all that you are, to live in
Heaven on Earth here and now.**

Things are going to unfold for you. Perfectly. Let everything be choiceless, easy, effortless, harmonious. You stay in the flow and let it all come to you. You stay in the flow and let it come to you. We assure you it will.

Anything you're trying to figure out, *anything* you're trying to make a decision about, let it go. *Let it play out.* Let yourself really see what this is all about. Live with no doubt. You can live in any reality you choose. Breathe yourself into the fullness of all that you are and all that is here for you.

Masters live for themselves and know that in doing so they serve the highest good, the divine plan. That does not mean that a master lives selfishly, because the master does not have a personal agenda. The master lives within their own experience and all that is available to them. The master owns no one. The master owes no one. The master allows All That Is. The master allows the energy and the light to guide the way. The master *follows* the energy, and when there is no energy, the master knows to *stop*.

**Follow the energy, and when there is no energy,
stop and allow the light to guide the way.**

If there's no energy, then there's nothing for you to do and no place for you to go. It is about you being in the fullness of who and where you are right here, right now, until there is a *clear* flow of energy, and then you allow it to guide the way. Many people distinctly try to *push* the energy when the energy has stopped. The master knows to stop when there is no energy.

When the energy is not guiding you to a new place to live, when the energy is not guiding you to a new relationship, when the energy is not guiding you to a new job or a new business, just stop. There's a reason. There's something coming in for you. There's something happening for you. There's more going on than you can see. *Isn't that good to know?*

You really only need inspired action about 3 percent of the time. That is all. So then you ask, *what is it that we are to do with all of our other time?* Do the things that bring you joy. Do the things that are fun for you. Create, play, have fun. Love, love, love. Love the trees. Love the land. Love the animals. Love the sun. Love yourself. Love your friends. Love your family. Love, experience joy, have fun, and appreciate beauty. Live life to the fullest. Be all that you are. Breathe in your well-being. Breathe. That's what you do.

Now, you might think that what we are saying about not having a personal agenda, allowing it all to come to you, following the energy, living as the master that you are, and being on this journey of the master means that you don't do great things or means that you're not a leader. It means *exactly* that you are doing great things. It means *exactly* that you are a leader. It means *exactly* that you're making a positive impact on the world around you. You are placed precisely where you are needed most because infinite intelligence knows who you are and knows what you know, which is how to live as a master and a wayshower in this time of the Great Awakening, which is why you are *here*.

Do you remember? Do you remember who you are? *Who am I? Who am I? Who am I?* Remember who you are. Remember how important you are. Remember why you're here. And hold the vision. Create it for yourself. Live it now. *Choose* it now. *Allow* it. *Be* it.

You are already seeing the vision move into manifested form, into your creation, faster than ever before. That is the acceleration. That is the quickening. As you elevate your vibration and your frequency, creation and manifestation happen almost instantly. This will help you understand why you step into lower dimensions of consciousness and why you stay there until you reach a level of impeccable creative expression dedicated to the highest good of all. You do it because the master in you knows the power you have to draw to you, through your force field. The master in you knows more of what you are and knows that your *consciousness* of all that you are, your consciousness of the vision you hold, your consciousness of a grander perspective, moves energy into form at an unprecedented rate for the realization of the highest good.

———

Remember, you are the Creator within your own creation. It is all created. It is all here and now.

———

Remember yourself as the Creator within your own creation. There is no *out there*. It is all a figment of your creation—what you have focused on, the vision that you've held, the consciousness that you've allowed, the energy that is flowing through you, a result of your creation. You get to play with all that is, all that was, all that will ever be. It is all created. It is all here and now. You just get to put it into some enjoyable, purposeful, fun, exciting, inspiring use in your own experience of form. And when you come to enjoy the fullness of your *formless* creations *at the same level of fulfillment* as your creations that are in form, you will then experience an even richer, fuller, grander reality.

Your perspective shifts when you elevate your consciousness and awareness, which is what we are doing with you right here, right now. While our words are important, this is a vibrational experience. Our words are important because they are expanding your consciousness and your awareness of the potentials and the possibilities that exist here for you beyond the limitation that you have learned. As we elevate your consciousness and awareness through our words, you're allowing a vibration and a frequency. You're allowing yourself to be in a higher vibration, to stay there longer, and to always remember how to get back to that place.

While our words are important, this is a vibrational experience, which is creating a new perspective, a new level of focus.

The way you perceive your experience creates your reality. Your perception creates your reality. So much more is possible for you when you remember that there is a force field of creation, that the energy that creates worlds is always flowing and is available to you at all times, and that through your *being* you draw more of what you *are* to you. When you expand your consciousness and awareness and expand your potential and look at things differently, perceive things differently, focus on a higher vision for your own experience, you build bridges to Heaven on Earth.

You're a bridge. You're a bridge. You're a bridge to the Promised Land.

If you are reading this, you have a dream in your heart. Every single one of you has a dream in your heart, even if you have forgotten it, even if at times it was too painful to remember. You came here with a dream in your heart. *You* placed that dream in your heart. It's there for a reason. It's time to let yourself experience it, the fullness, the richness of all that you are. And so it is. And so it is.

———

You placed that dream in your heart.
It's time to let yourself experience it.

———

ESSENTIAL MESSAGES

- The question you asked that started this entire awakening experience for you was the question, *who am I?*

- The master of one's life is no longer trying to create from lack or limitation or unworthiness. The master has no personal agenda.

- People are changed by many events, but it's not the chaos that changes them. It's not the fear that changes them. It is the *love* that changes them.

- There are no big decisions you need to make except for the simple decision to open and allow energy, to be all that you are, to live in Heaven on Earth here and now.

- The master *follows* the energy, and when there is no energy, the master knows to *stop*.

- In the doing, there's always more to be done. In the *being*, all things are done through you.

- Through your *being* you draw more of what you *are* to you. When you expand your consciousness and awareness and expand your potential and look at things differently, perceive things differently, and focus on a higher vision for your own experience, you build bridges to Heaven on Earth.

CHAPTER TWELVE

THE POWERFUL CREATOR THAT YOU ARE

**In this chapter, The Council expresses what it means
to be a master within the human experience, playing and
having fun as you create the reality you choose for you.**

We are so pleased and delighted to be in the presence of you, dear master. You are The Council here on Earth, and so it is. You are The Council here on Earth. You are here because you focused yourself into this level of consciousness known as the Earth Experiment, known as the Earth Experience. *You* focused yourself here. *You* chose this experience for you. If you can choose the very thing to have this experience of life—the consciousness that you are in form—and you can create the entire experience of being human and experience yourself as a personality, then you can focus yourself into *any* creation of reality you choose.

You are The Council here on Earth.

You believe this all to be real and, well, it is. There is so much more that is also real. You are fully stepping into the realization of all that you are, and with it you will accelerate, amplify, and ascend your own physical experience into a reality that you have only imagined, only dreamed of, only known somewhere within you is possible. There is *so much more*. If you are reading this, you can accept the truth that you are a master. Otherwise, you would not be reading it.

We are not saying that you are better than anyone else. We are not saying that this is a hierarchical advantage over anyone because you are somehow better than another. That is not why we use the word *master*. You are a *master* because you have mastered a certain level of consciousness, awareness, energy, vibration, thought forms, and creation, so that you could come into the full realization of allowing all that you are. You remember that you possess the freedom to *choose* for yourself any reality, any experience, and the creative expression of all that you are.

You never needed more money to create. You never needed some particular person to help you. You never needed a certain level of physicality to be able to do it. All you needed was the consciousness and the awareness to open and allow the energy that has always been here for you to take *any* form within your own creation, for it to be everything that you intended it to be.

It is so easy to give it away, but all of your power is for *you*. Your power does not work for someone else. Someone else's power does not work for you. But, oh, when you come together as the master that you are with another who is also in the realization of the master that they are, and you begin to play and have fun with all of creation—oh, *that*, our dear masters, is so *very* exciting.

You are pioneers of new energy and new consciousness and new potentials and new possibilities. You are the pioneers. You are the bridge builders. You are the guides stepping into higher levels of consciousness and learning how to navigate new energy and new consciousness in the most extraordinary ways—but you're doing so in ways that are fun and creative and playful.

*You are guides learning to navigate energy
and consciousness in extraordinary,
fun, creative, playful ways.*

Some of you—and we do not understand, although there is no judgment from our side ever, because we know it's just a level of consciousness you're in—still choose to work and force and try to figure it out and effort it and push energy instead of just getting into the new energy and the new consciousness, playing and creating and having fun. There's never been a better time. There's never been a better you. Sure, there are some in your world who would say, *it is not a good time to create, not a good time to play, not a good time to have fun,* but that has nothing to do with you. That's the reality they are choosing for themselves based on the level of consciousness they are in.

We do not say this with any judgment because we know you're all going to get there. We know everyone's going to get there in their own time, in their own way. Truth is truth is truth. You will all return to the truth of who you are. It's just *so much more fun* when you really allow yourself to be all that you are and to open to the power that you are. Don't give your power to the media. Don't give your power to the television. Don't give your power to the politicians. Don't give your power to anything outside of you. All of the energy is here for you to create the experience that you choose for you.

When you really understand that, there is no *need* to go into fear, to go into suffering, to go into worry, to go into powerlessness. There is no more need for it. Was there ever a need for it? Does all experience provide data and information? Indeed. But you think you came here for the limitation. You didn't. You came here for the expansion. You just weren't *afraid* of anything that existed within the whole of the human experience. Why? Because you never intended to forget that you could choose the creation that *you* most wanted to experience for you, and that even if there were just a few people living at the level of experience that you choose for you, well, that would be more than enough. The more you live there, and the more you come together, and the more you allow the fullness of all that you are, and the more you choose and live within your creation of your reality, the more you will realize that drawing others into your field is *merely* an experience of focusing. In your focus and your choosing, you draw to you the particles that create the experience of another and others and all sorts of incredible things in your field.

You have been asking, *How do we turn particles into form?* In order to accomplish or realize what it is you're asking, you must understand what you *are*. You are consciousness focused through your own choosing in the human experience. You are consciousness, and you knew coming in, as the consciousness that you are, that this experience would expand you, expand consciousness, expand the human experience, and expand the consciousness that's in the human experience.

You focused yourself into this experience, into the consciousness of the Earth Plane, knowing that you were always, always able to open and allow energy to serve you in the fulfillment of everything you could ever need in this experience—infinite intelligence, infinite love, infinite abundance, infinite well-being. You focused yourself into this experience knowing that you always had the energy that creates worlds available to you, flowing to you, an *infinite* supply of everything you could ever need and more available to you in every moment. You were not afraid to come here or entangle with any of the limitations that existed in this experience because you knew. You knew when you came here and you knew when you opened your eyes that you were perceiving in a field of consciousness.

In time, you entangled and entangled and entangled more deeply in the human consciousness and the limitation there within, and you began to identify yourself and what was possible for you simply based on that—what others told you was possible, what others experienced, which came from their beliefs in their own possibility. You began to buy into all these things that are merely another's creation based on their beliefs in their own limitation. There's something within you—or you wouldn't be reading this—that has always known that more was possible for you than you ever were told. There was a knowing within you of who you are and that there were other ways; there were many ways. There are many ways to truth.

Everyone's journey through this experience of expansion and expression and creation is perfect. Whatever another is choosing has nothing to do with you unless you entangle with it through your focus on it. Your focus on fear, your focus on judgment, your focus on those who are lower in dimensions of consciousness entangles you with it. Your focus on higher-level consciousness, your focus on joy and play and fun entangles you with that. Your focus on infinite intelligence is what moves it into form. Consciousness is what moves energy into form. Energy responds to consciousness, to focus.

———

Your focus on higher-level consciousness, joy, play, and fun entangles you with that and moves it into form. Energy responds to focus.

———

You're here to create based on your choosing, but you never, ever had to move into density in order to create that which you choose for you. You just get tangled up in expectations, specificness, limitation, separation, and you then take a very difficult road through the idea of manifestation. But that's what many of you were ready for next. That's what opened you up to another state of awareness, and that's what opened up another state of consciousness. Now you're ready for more, and beyond this there will be more as well. It just gets better. It just gets better, but it comes down to the thoughts that you are thinking, what you are focused on, what you're giving your attention to. Your *perception* is what creates your reality. How you're perceiving is what is creating your reality, is what is drawing to you in your field the very experience that you are choosing through your focus and your intention.

You really can't get this wrong. We say, *master impeccable creative expression dedicated to the highest good,* which doesn't mean that you're creating something that will fix everybody else. It means that you're creating in a way that *does no harm* to another. However, you creating and choosing for you in a field of limitless potential might move you out of an experience of someone else's force field that is entangled with fear and judgment and limitation, and you might think there's harm there because you moved out of each other's experiences. But it's not that you harmed them. Their belief in things that are not true about who they are creates their own suffering within the experience of your expanded force field (which is moving in a different direction).

No direction is right or wrong. But when you believe that you could ever unlove anyone or anything, it is a very simple mistruth and misunderstanding of who and what you are. There is only love. There is no separation, not through time, space, history, or geography. There is no separation. It just exists as something within a lower dimension of consciousness that never quite feels right to you.

Mastering impeccable creative expression in the highest good of all is simply understanding that you create with such impeccable innocence and ease that you do not harm yourself or any other. To harm even on some level implies that the change of form of something could be the end, which again is simply not true. Nothing is ever destroyed. No energy is ever destroyed. You cannot destroy energy. It just changes form. It just changes form. It's always going to change form. Everything is always changing form. That is creation. That's a wonderful thing. When you know you can navigate through creation—which sounds better than change—when you know you can navigate through creation with ease and grace in the most impeccable way, *then you know* you can play and create and have so much fun here.

When you want to move particles into form, we want you to see it for what it really is. You are a force field of consciousness focused in the physical experience. Your consciousness is the depth and breadth of your field. The more conscious you are, the more aware you are. In higher dimensions of consciousness, there's more potential. There are more possibilities because in your elevated consciousness you have raised your vibration and expanded your force field of creation, which is you. You are a force field of energy. You are a force field of creation. In the most innocent, impeccable, joyful, fun, playful, exciting way, you draw creation to you. You *focus on* that which you draw into your experience, and that focus is what draws the particles into your field so that you experience them as form within creation. But don't just limit it to the form.

———

You are a force field of energy, and you draw creation into your experience through your focus.

———

Yes, there is great fulfillment within the human experience of being able to touch and hear and feel and kiss and love and hold and drive and ride and *live* and all the other things you do. It's wonderful. It's wonderful. We want you to experience the fullness. We have said live your life fully, whatever that means to you. Love fully. Be all that you are. Choose and create and experience more. You just don't need to move anything into lack and separation and frustration and being so specific and difficult. That causes resistance such that you then find yourself in the lack of it, the limitation, the suffering, the struggle. When that's what you're focused on, you move yourself into a reality of limitation. You get more of what you focus on, whether it is wanted or unwanted.

You're always choosing. You just aren't always conscious of the choices you can make. You just haven't been conscious of your full potential. You haven't been conscious of all the possibilities. They've been here all along, you just weren't aware of them. Now you're becoming aware of your potential. It's not that any one creation is better than the other, but when you align with the I Am Creator frequency, the attachment to some specific car or person or amount of money or amount of followers or amount of fans or some perfect image of something is suddenly not as interesting and exciting as the *awareness of your greater potential and possibilities* as the Creator within your own creation.

The I Am Creator frequency is not one of trying to figure out how to move particles of money into form so you will have enough to pay the bills. That is not the I Am Creator frequency. That is: *I am in lack and limitation and I need to figure out how to push energy into some form so that I feel better, because I'm not enough, I don't have enough, and I don't have access to the infinite abundance that I knew was always available to me when I focused myself into this human experience.*

Now, is that a form of creation? Yes. Is it a fun one? No— unless you *like* playing the game of not having enough so that you can see your power to "get by," and draw it to you just in the nick of time.

What game do you want to play here? You're in the human experience. You're in the human experiment. What game do you want to play? Do you want to play the game of your ultimate potential? Do you want to play games with infinite intelligence and infinite love and infinite abundance and infinite well-being? Or do you want to play the game of *I don't have the power to say no, so I'm going to blame it on my body not being able to heal just so that I don't have to tell them that I don't want to do that because I don't believe that I have the power?*

Now, there's no judgment from our side. All of your games, all of your experiences are perfect, and there's no judgment from our side ever. We love you so much, but you wouldn't have drawn this information to you if you weren't asking for what is next. *What's really possible for me? Who am I?* Until the answer to that is "I Am Creator," you're still not fully stepping into the realization of all that you are. The master knows that they can live a really big life within ultimate simplicity. They can live their fullness and the full creation of all that they are in a state of peace and harmony and well-being in any experience they choose.

We want you to get beyond the judgment of what you choose for you. We want you to get beyond the judgment of your own creations or anyone else's. Get beyond the judgment of whatever you created or think you miscreated in the past. It's not here now, it's not who you are, and it's not the power and potential that is available to you in every moment. The master knows one of the greatest creations of all is stillness and the joy of stillness and the beauty of stillness. The master knows that one of the greatest creations of all is dancing with All That Is, being in the flow and in the stillness in this dance of creation with All That Is, no matter where you are.

Whether your idea of Heaven on Earth is in a home with a big family and a lot of people and a lot going on and a lot of noise, of you in a beautiful little cabin in the middle of the forest where the majority of your day is spent in nature with the animals, of you traveling the world with all sorts of adventures with new people and new cultures and new experiences, or of a partnership of two masters exploring deeper levels of love and expansion within a creation—it's all perfect. *Just choose it.*

Just choose it. Get aligned to the Creator that you are and allow your force field of expansion to span this entire planet so that it draws what it is that you choose to you from your field of creation. When you limit yourself and you limit your power, your force field shrinks. You go into resistance, and you contract the field. You pull it all in, make it really, really small, and then you wonder why you feel like you have to push and force energy and make it happen in your time and your way.

It's all done if you choose it. It can all be done if you choose it.

We're going to have some *fun* here once you really step into being the true realized masters that you are, when the conversations are no longer about your lack and separation and your fear and your worry because you *know* the powerful Creator that you are. Then your questions are going to be, *What's possible now? Who am I, this I Am Creator?* You will experience yourself as the Creator that you are, the Creator within your own creation, the fully realized master of your own life. Then it's about fun and play and creating, because there's infinite well-being here, there's infinite abundance here, there's infinite love here, and there is infinite intelligence that is always available to you. All that's asked, *all that's asked* is for you to allow the energy of the I Am Creator frequency that's been here for you all along. You are not allowing energy when you are trying to figure it out, when you're trying to push energy into something that *seems* like it *should* be what you're supposed to do.

———

When you experience yourself as the fully realized master that you are, it's about play and creating, because there is infinite intelligence available to you.

———

There are many questions about service and contribution, about being the wayshowers and the guides that you are. It's inevitable, but you still take on service like it's a job you are to do, instead of stepping into the fully realized master that you are in the I Am Creator frequency, opening and allowing energy to serve you, following the light, and then doing what is fun for *you*, doing what brings *you* joy, expressing yourself in ways that are beautiful and fun and creative for *you*. Know that in doing that you will serve in the most incredible ways and that you will create a ripple effect that is felt throughout this entire human existence because one more of you stepped into realization, one more of you realized your own enlightenment, one more of you chose Heaven on Earth.

The sounds of Heaven on Earth get louder. The beauty within Heaven on Earth gets brighter. That's what's meant by being a beacon of light or shining your light. The more of you who step into Heaven on Earth, the more it is heard, the more it is seen, the more it is felt, and the more it begins to be *understood* as a potential and a possibility for any and all of those who choose it. *That* is contribution. That is service without trying to force and effort and work to figure it out.

You would all say, *I really want to trust that this all works. I really want to trust that infinite intelligence and infinite well-being and infinite abundance and infinite love are there for me.* To trust is to know the truth, and when it is truth there's no longer a need to trust. It is the truth. Truth is truth. Truth is truth. There are many ways, but the truth of who you really are and what is possible for you and why you're here is the truth, whether you allow it or you hold yourself in the separation of it.

When we say *separation*, we mean that the experience of separation within the Third Dimension is that each of you are separate, that you're separate from God, that you're separate from Source, that you're separate from the money you want, you're separate from the lover you want, you're separate from the health that you want, you're separate from the cure to your disease, you're separate from the job that will make you happy. You've all been there, and you've all done that. You've all been on that journey before. There's nothing wrong with it. There's no judgment from our side ever, but *you* drew this to you because you chose *more*. You *chose* a grander potential. You *chose* to elevate your consciousness. You *chose* to raise your vibration. You chose. You chose you. You choosing you is the best thing you can do for anybody because you choosing you expands the force field of creation that is you, and you choosing you expands the potentials and the possibilities, expands the energy that you're allowing, expands everything in the experience of you.

The very best thing you can do is choose *you*, because in that, you allow more love through you, more harmony, more peace, more joy, more abundance, more well-being. You allow more of all that you are because you *are* the infinite intelligence, you *are* the infinite abundance, you *are* the infinite well-being, and you *are* the infinite love. That is what you *are*. So you choosing you allows more of what you are. The rest will come into alignment with where you are, and if it doesn't, you don't *want* to go back into the old way of trying to negotiate lower vibrations. You don't. You don't have to. That was a belief in limitation or that somehow the way you served people was to go down into the trauma and drama and suffer with them and drag them out of it at the expense of your own vibration. You pay a vibrational price to entangle with what is *not* the truth of you.

When you believe you have no power to choose for you, you say things like: *Well, I have to go spend time with that person. Oh, I have to go to that thing. I have to go here. I have to do that.* What you are actually saying is, *I don't have the power to choose for me.* When you say *I have to* or *I should*, we want you to know what you're really saying is *I don't have the power to choose for me.*

That is going to feel really awful, because nothing, *nothing,* could be further from the truth. You *do* have the power to choose for you. You are the power that creates, which means you *are* the power. You are the I Am Creator frequency. When you say, *I have to go over and do this for this person,* you're saying, *I don't have the power to choose for me. I don't have the power to choose.* Then you wonder why your body entangles with diseases and all sorts of things where you must be on a certain diet because you don't have the power to metabolize certain things anymore. It is because you moved yourself into an experience of not having the power— because you said, *I have to do this. I don't have the power. I don't have the power to choose.*

———

Experience the truth of who you are. You are the power. You have the power to choose for you.

———

We hope you see this with such perfection, without any judgment, because there is none. If you're in judgment, it's just because you're creating it through your own judgment of yourself. There's no judgment here from our side ever, but we think you're really asking to experience the truth of who you are now that you have remembered that *you* are The Council here on Earth. You're the pioneers. You're the wayshowers. You're the ones who are going to do great things within human potential and possibilities. You are the potential. You are the possibility of what true realized *power* can create in an easy, effortless, harmonious, impeccable way, where there's no need to entangle with limitation and therefore do harm to yourself or any other.

It's all perfect from our side. At times you may say, *I have to go do this job because I don't have the power to draw infinite abundance to me.* Or you may find yourself thinking the following: *I have to stay at this job because it is my source. I don't have the power to align to my own source, because through my thinking and my thoughts I'm judging myself and shaming myself and seeing myself as a failure and not good enough. There must be something I have to fix. There must be something I'm doing wrong. There must be something wrong with me.* When you do this, you're actually saying, *I'm not the god of me. I'm not the master. I'm not the power. I'm not all of this that I know myself to be.* You are actually so powerful that you can draw yourself into the experience of powerlessness, and then in your powerlessness you shut down your ability to be all that you are, which is the very infinite intelligence that is you.

The thoughts you're thinking are affecting the way that you feel, which is affecting your vibration, which is determining what you are creating within your reality, which determines what you're drawing to you, which determines the experience you're having.

You don't have time—although there is no time—to worry anymore. You don't have it, because you have the whole rest of your life to play and create and have fun and experience yourself as the infinite being that you are. What are you choosing? What are you focused on? That's what you're voting for, and that's what you're getting more of.

———

You have the rest of your life to play and create and have fun and experience yourself as the infinite being that you are.

———

There's no need to worry about anything ever again. There's nothing to fear. In every moment, you can open up to energy, which will *always* lead you and guide you, and that energy is what brings the infinite supply of everything you could need and more. You don't ever have to worry about anything ever again. You don't ever have to judge anyone else's experience ever again because you are the Creator within your own creation. You don't have to figure anything out *ever again* because you can just allow the energy and the light to guide the way with effortless ease. You don't need to suffer. You don't need to struggle. You don't need chaos or drama or trauma.

Your ascension to higher dimensions of consciousness, and therefore elevated experiences of reality knowing yourself as the I Am Creator frequency, is here for you *now*. And so it is. All you need to do is choose it, and then choose it again, and choose it again, and choose it again. Your thoughts are what you are choosing, every time. When you're in judgment, that's what you're choosing. When you're worrying, that's what you're choosing. When you think you're not enough or the Source that created worlds and the universe and you has somehow forgotten about you, even though it is you, it couldn't be. That's why it feels so awful to think that way. It is simply not true, and that's why it feels so awful. It always has felt that awful. You've just been on the other side now, so it seems more awful than ever before.

You have felt pure bliss. You have expanded into greater perspectives. You've allowed yourself, even if just for a few moments, to be totally satiated and to come into balance with peace and harmony and the fullness of all that you are. Believing things that are not true is going to feel more awful than ever before. Those are your moments to catch it and *choose* for you, the I Am Creator that you *are*.

No, there's not a lack of time, really, but why, *why* would you choose anything other than playing, creating, having fun, being in joy, being in peace, being in harmony, dancing with all of creation, feeling into the freedom to choose the life you want to live, living fully, loving fully? We just don't know why. And there's no judgment from our side ever.

This is what's real. *This is what's real.* This is the truth within you that you've always known. If you've heard us many times or you're hearing us for the first time, you drew this to you because you are ready to hear it and remember it *now*. You have a clean slate, a fresh start, a perfect opportunity, the best time ever, here and now. Choose for you. Choose for you.

———

**You have expanded into a greater perspective.
You have a clean slate, a fresh start, a perfect
opportunity. Choose for you.**

———

We are here on our side because we promised we would be, so that you would never forget this truth within you that you know. Now let the journey, this journey, unfold with ease and grace. Get excited about it. Play, have fun. Your perfection is not required. Never was. Just let it be easier. Just move into creation energy and let a beautiful, expansive, exciting reality present itself to you.

We have shared a great amount of information with you, and there is so much more to come. We remind you that you are everything you wish to be. You already are. We love you, we love you, *we love you*. And with that, we are complete.

ESSENTIAL MESSAGES

- Everyone's journey through this experience of expansion and expression and creation is perfect, is just as it should be.

- Don't give your power to anything outside of you. All the energy is here for you to create the experience that you choose for you.

- Your perception is what creates your reality. It comes down to the thoughts that you are thinking, what you are focused on, what you're giving your attention to.

- We're going to have some fun here once you really step into the true realized masters that you are, when the conversations are no longer about your lack and separation and your fear and your worry because you *know* the powerful Creator that you are.

- The very best thing you can do is choose *you*, because in that, you allow more love to permeate your life, more harmony to be your experience, more peace, more joy, more abundance, more well-being.

- You don't have to figure anything out ever again because you can just *allow* the energy and the light to guide the way with effortless ease.

AFTERWORD

There is a purpose for you. There is a purpose to all of
this. There is a potential here for the most incredible
transformation of human consciousness that has ever
occurred in any lifetime. There is a reason for humanity
to awaken, because on the other side of an awakened
human family is a grander potential for Earth and all its
inhabitants, in this vast and glorious universe.

— THE COUNCIL

It's common to, after reading such profound, inspiring material, ask the question, "What am I supposed to do now?"

Many people experience profound and life-changing transformations after being introduced to The Council. Things change—relationships, circumstances, perspectives, desires, and so much more. Some feel an insatiable desire to discover their greater calling, some are called to immerse themselves in spiritual teachings, and yet others feel the guidance to learn how to develop their own channel so that they can tap into infinite wisdom anytime they wish.

No matter what occurs, trust that everything is happening for you. Trust that you will receive everything that you need. You have drawn this book to you in divine right time, for the perfect unfolding of your destiny. Remember that from a state of being, all things will be done through you. Let the perfect next step come to you. Follow the energy and let the light guide the way forward. Let it be easy and effortless.

When you feel yourself in resistance, trying to figure things out, or in a state of overwhelm, take three deep breaths and come back into the now moment. All your power is in this now moment. Then ask yourself, "What would bring more joy, more love, more freedom, or more peace right now?"

Have fun with all of this—play, laugh, create, explore, and imagine the possibilities. Allow yourself to integrate this wisdom, day by day, in the most enjoyable ways for you. And most of all, be gentle with yourself.

This is a book you will want to read time and time again. I recommend that you flip to a chapter or a page each day and simply read the words you are being guided to in that moment. Each time, you will discover new things and cultivate a deeper understanding of the wisdom within you. As The Council tells us, this is your wisdom. Read it, sit with it, and ask your higher self for guidance and clarity. Ask for things to be choiceless as you navigate through life's experiences. Remember, you are The Council here on Earth, and your life is meant to be so, so very good for you.

You truly are everything you wish to be. It is all within you and it has always been.

ABOUT THE AUTHOR

Sara Landon is a globally celebrated transformational leader, spiritual teacher, and channel of The Council. She has been called a "leader of leaders for the next generation of teachers, wayshowers, channels, coaches, and guides" who are contributing to raising the consciousness of the planet. Passionate about living her highest potential, Sara shines a light on the path for others to expand beyond the perceived limitations of the human experience and live as the realized masters that they are.

As the voice of The Council, Sara's intention is to be the purest channel of their wisdom and teachings, which offer a grander perspective of what is possible for each of us—and our beloved human family—as we elevate our consciousness to new levels. She focuses herself, as the ultimate student, to live their teachings at the highest level and is dedicated to helping others discover that they too can connect to these greater levels of awareness and guidance.

Sara is unique in the field of channeling in that she not only shares The Council's wisdom but offers revolutionary guidance on how to apply and integrate their teachings in everyday life for more joy, peace, ease, love, freedom, beauty, and abundance.

A powerful luminary, Sara's greatest joy is helping those who are ready to play in new levels of energy reconnect with all that they are so they may live, love, and lead in this time of awakening. Sara holds the vision of a fully awakened world where all beings coexist harmoniously with one another and with Earth. Through courses, coaching groups, and activations, as well as her Global Masters Class program, she has helped thousands around the world integrate the wisdom of The Council.

For more information and resources, please visit: saralandon.com.

We hope you enjoyed this Hay House book. If you'd like to receive our online catalog featuring additional information on Hay House books and products, or if you'd like to find out more about the Hay Foundation, please contact:

Hay House, Inc., P.O. Box 5100, Carlsbad, CA 92018-5100
(760) 431-7695 or (800) 654-5126
(760) 431-6948 (fax) or (800) 650-5115 (fax)
www.hayhouse.com® • www.hayfoundation.org

———

Published in Australia by: Hay House Australia Pty. Ltd.,
18/36 Ralph St., Alexandria NSW 2015
Phone: 612-9669-4299 • *Fax:* 612-9669-4144
www.hayhouse.com.au

Published in the United Kingdom by: Hay House UK, Ltd.,
The Sixth Floor, Watson House, 54 Baker Street, London W1U 7BU
Phone: +44 (0)20 3927 7290 • *Fax:* +44 (0)20 3927 7291
www.hayhouse.co.uk

Published in India by: Hay House Publishers India,
Muskaan Complex, Plot No. 3, B-2, Vasant Kunj, New Delhi 110 070
Phone: 91-11-4176-1620 • *Fax:* 91-11-4176-1630
www.hayhouse.co.in

———

Access New Knowledge.
Anytime. Anywhere.

Learn and evolve at your own pace
with the world's leading experts.

www.hayhouseU.com